INCREASE
MY
FAITH

C. Michael Patton

Credo House

INCREASE MY FAITH
© 2011 by C. Michael Patton
All rights reserved.

ISBN: 1463761759
ISBN-13: 978-1463761752

Printed in the United States of America.

Credo House
PUBLISHERS
www.credohouse.org

ENDORSEMENTS:

As I began to read Michael Patton's text *Increase My Faith*, I quickly grew intrigued. Then I found myself drawn into his carefully-delineated concepts regarding the nature of faith. I was especially intrigued by his repeated depictions of his "Belief-O-Meter"—what an original and helpful aide to illustrating these thoughts! Moreover, the practical implications of these thoughts for personal belief, handling one's doubts, and so on that are found on almost every page combine to make this volume a very valuable resource.

Gary R. Habermas, Distinguished Research Professor, *Liberty Baptist Theological Seminary*

"C. Michael Patton has provided us with a rich, intelligent guide to faith. Besides the clarity of writing and practicality, the strength of the book resides in the very careful distinctions Patton makes, along with his identification of the real-life implications of those distinctions. This is an important book and I highly recommend it."

J. P. Moreland, Distinguished Professor of Philosophy, *Talbot School of Theology* and author of *The God Question*

"Lord, I believe. Help my unbelief!" If this is the cry of your heart, you need to read this book. Michael Patton provides an engaging and informative look at the nature of true faith. Along the way, he illuminates the aspects of belief and conviction that facilitate spiritual growth. Highly recommended.

Trevin Wax, author of *Counterfeit Gospels* and *Holy Subversion*, editor of TGM (Theology, Gospel, Mission) at LifeWay Christian Resources

We live in days of doubt. The unrelenting barrage of skepticism and uncertainty has left many feeling like the man who cried out to Jesus, "I do believe; help my unbelief." This book is a welcome, thoughtful answer to that age-old request. I have known Michael Patton for almost thirty years, and I can't think of a more spiritually qualified person to write this book. His own faith has been severely tested and refined in the crucible of deeply trying times. I have watched his faith grow, and it has blessed my life. Read this book to inform and increase your faith.

Mark Hitchcock, Pastor, Faith Bible Church, Edmond, OK; Author *The Complete Book of Bible Prophecy*

"We live in a time when almost everyone claims to value 'faith' but few know what faith in God really means. Michael Patton's book Increase My Faith takes a classic Christian understanding of faith and gives it fresh and creative expression with what he calls the Belief-o-Meter. This book will be encouraging and illuminating for anyone who needs to increase in faith or know someone who does."

Robert M Bowman, Author *Putting Jesus in His Place: The Case for the Deity of Christ*

"I have watched people all over the country stop and listen when Michael Patton speaks on the issue of faith. Michael authentically speaks from both disciplined study and places of significant pain. I am blessed to know Michael 'close-up' and I testify to you he lives out the important message found in this book. I pray the Lord would use *Increase My Faith* to deepen the faith of our Savior's Bride. I recommend it without hesitation."

Tim Kimberley, Executive Director, *Credo House Ministries*

To my dear wife Kristie who is the most loyal rock in my life.

TABLE OF CONTENTS

INTRODUCTION		8
1:	FAITH CUBED	14
2:	KNOWING WHAT YOU BELIEVE	22
3:	KNOW WHY YOU BELIEVE	32
4:	CONVICTION	42
5:	REFERRED CONVICTION	50
6:	RATIONAL CONVICTION	60
7:	ADDING EVIDENCE TO OUR CONVICTION	72
8:	FIRST-HAND FAITH	82
9:	FORENSIC EVIDENCE FOR CHRIST AND FOR THE DEATH OF MY SISTER	92
10:	FAITH IS A DECISION	106
11:	FIXING OUR FAITH	120
APPENDIX A: HOW TO STUDY THE BIBLE IN A NUTSHELL		130
APPENDIX B: ARGUMENTS FOR THE EXISTENCE OF GOD IN A NUTSHELL		142
APPENDIX C: ARGUMENTS FOR THE RESURRECTION OF CHRIST IN A NUTSHELL		146

INCREASE MY FAITH

INTRODUCTION

"And the apostles said to the Lord, 'Increase our faith!'" (Luke 17:5). Here the disciples are with Jesus Christ in their very presence and they request that their faith be increased. All of us need stronger faith today than we had yesterday. All of us need to turn to the Lord daily and make this same request.

Faith. It goes by many names: faith, belief, confidence, trust, assurance, dependence, certainty. But what is faith? I have asked many people this question: What does it mean to believe? Normally, the first answer I get is, "Believe what?" Now *that* is a good question. You can't just believe without believing *in* something. Others just replace it with a synonym. "It means to be faithful." "It means to trust." Others take it to the next level: "It means to obey." Some of the more determined say, "It means that you *know* something to be true."

Defining faith is discipleship 101. Every believer should know exactly what faith is. Unfortunately, more often than not, when I ask this question of well-meaning Christians, they say something like this: "It means to believe something *no matter what*." No matter what? But

INTRODUCTION

what if that something does not deserve our belief? What if the evidence is not there? What if the evidence is actually *against* it? "That is what faith is," they respond, "the blinder the better."

I am reminded of one of my all-time favorite movies, *Indiana Jones and the Last Crusade*. You remember: Indiana Jones, the great explorer, was in search of the Holy Grail. Desperate to find it, as it held the only hope for his dying father's survival, Indy made his way through a series of three tests. Having easily deciphered the first two, he faced the greatest test of all, "the test of faith." There he stood, at the edge of a canyon with no visible way across. The only thing that separated him from the cave in which the Holy Grail resided was a great gulf. However, the requirement to pass was faith. More specifically, the instructions from his father's Grail journal said that he must take a "leap of faith." It was now or never. Time was running out. Indy had to make the move. Finally, he closed his eyes, stuck his left leg out, and took the leap. Suddenly, his foot found solid footing in a bridge that was camouflaged before, but could be seen now that he was on it.

Is this what God is asking us to do? Is this what the Christian life is all about? Are we to close our eyes, stick out our leg, and hope our foot finds firm grounding? *What does it mean to believe?*

Faith is at the heart of the Christian message. It is what begins the Christian life and it is what defines the Christian life – so much so that Christians are often referred to as "believers."

1 Thessalonians 2:13
And we also thank God constantly for this, that when you received the word of God, which you heard from us, you accepted it not as the word of men but as what it really is, the word of God, which is at work in you *believers*. (emphasis mine)

Why are we called believers? Just because we have a propensity for belief? No. It is because we believe God. Belief is not just something that we have done in the past, but something that we do *now*. God has introduced himself to us through the Gospel message, and we counted him trustworthy – worthy of our reliance. We have confidence that when he speaks, he speaks that which is in accordance with reality. We believe he knows what he is talking about. We believe that he knows more than us.

The motto at my ministry, the Credo House, is "Helping people to believe more accurately and more deeply today than they did yesterday." I love this motto. It expresses what I aspire to be and how I want to be used. It is about belief first. Without faith, all else matters little. There is an old saying: "You are what you eat." I often tell people that this is not true. It is not ultimately what you eat that makes you who you are (though eating healthfully is important); it is what you believe. You are what you believe.

However, I have come to find out over the years that belief is not as simple as I would like it to be. Rather, it can be very complex. I think most of us find this to be the case as we continue in our walk with God. As life's challenges surface, we begin to open our spiritual toolbox, looking for answers to our wayward thoughts and feelings, finding that we are unsure of exactly where the problem lies. The belief that came so easily before starts slipping away. Often it does not necessarily disappear, but changes and nuances itself – a metamorphosis. Either way, we find that belief is not as black and white as we once thought.

Questions such as these begin to arise:

- If I *really* believed, how could I have sinned in such a way?

- Have I ever *truly* believed, or am I just following in the tradition laid by my parents?

- If I believe, why do I have so much doubt? Does that mean I don't *really* believe?

- Is my belief purely emotional, without any rationale? Is this okay? Is belief supposed to be blind?

- Some days I believe, some days I don't. Why?

INTRODUCTION

- How much belief is necessary to be saved?

- What *exactly* do I have to believe?

Before long, we find ourselves confused and robbed of our security. We neither know what to believe or how to believe it.

However, while there is a complexity to belief, there is also a simplicity to it. Belief in Christ is so simple that Jesus himself said a child can do it (Mark 10:15). There is a "matter-of-factness" that the Bible presents when it comes to faith. Sometimes it seems that one either has it or they don't.

Getting caught up in its complexities can cause us to throw our hands up in the air and say, "What is it worth? I will just wait to see how it all turns out in the end." But this would amount to making a preliminary decision that the Bible does not support. In fact, this would be the very antinomy of what it means to believe as a Christian. While faith can be very complex, the Bible provides some foundations that stabilize our understanding and keep us from becoming too discouraged.

In this book, I am going to talk about the what? why? and how? of Christian belief. I am going to cover three components that faith must include in order to be true faith. This is a book that I wish I had early in my Christian walk. These three components of faith have revolutionized my thinking and my approach toward God. They have created the paradigm through which my spirituality is filtered.

This book is for anyone who wants to increase their faith in God. It is for those who doubt and don't know why. It is for those who seek to love God with all their being, but find something missing. It is for those who are confused about why they are not better Christians. Simply put, this book will serve as a faith diagnosis. Just as we go to the doctor, sometimes when we have a physical ailment and sometimes merely for a check-up, this book is for those who have a spiritual ailment or are due for their spiritual check-up. My prayer is that you finish this book with more confidence, hope, commitment, and peace, knowing that God not only desires your faith to be strong, but has given you the means to make it strong.

Notes:

CHAPTER #1

FAITH CUBED

The Belief-O-Meter

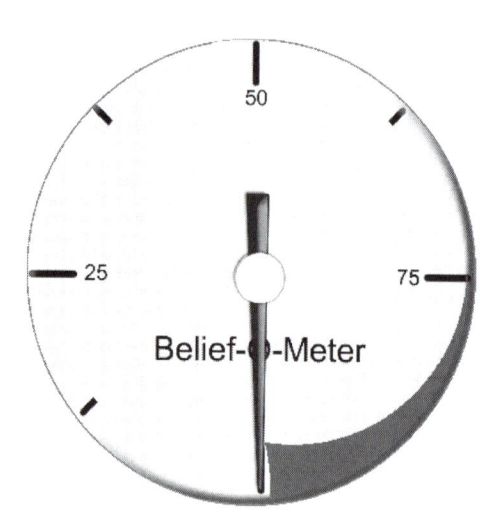

As you can see, the meter is set to zero. This means no faith is present at all. The further the dial goes to the right (like a speedometer in a car), the greater the faith. Once someone hits the "red zone", for lack of a better phrase, their faith is "on fire."

The first thing I want you to notice is that belief is not black and white. Don't miss this. The entire book is going to be based on this assumption. I remember many years ago, talking to a gentleman over lunch who had some problems with what I had written. His basic problem was that he believed faith is black or white.

CHAPTER 1: FAITH CUBED

You either have it or you don't. No in-between. I asked him if his faith was perfect. He said that it was not (and acted as if I had asked a crazy question). I then asked if his faith was perfect in any one area, say, his belief in the resurrection of Christ. Again, he answered no. I said, "So you are telling me that you can grow in your belief in Christ's resurrection. You are saying that you can believe more today than you did yesterday?" I think he got my point. It is pretty simple. Some people's faith is very strong. Some people's faith, though present, is weak. We are all going to find ourselves at various levels of belief. Our goal each day is to believe more today than we did yesterday. One day our belief will be perfected. Today, it is a work in progress.

On the meter, if someone is at 10, while this is a low "faith reading," they still have faith. It is only when the dial is at a zero that faith is not present. Some of us find ourselves with very little faith crying out to God, "I believe, help my unbelief!" (Mark 9:24). Our hopes are to have our faith as high as it can go, but in the words of my favorite philosopher Bono, some days are better than others.

Okay. Hang with me. We are going to add three "sub-meters" to our belief meter. These three additions are placed within the main meter, as they are meters upon which the main meter is dependant. These come from the great 16th century Reformers of the Protestant Reformation. Though primarily articulated through the writings of guy named Francis Turretin, the basic components are found throughout the history of Christian thought. Most succinctly, the Reformers said that in order to have true biblical faith, these three components must be present (forgive the fancy Latin titles; I only include them to look smarter):

1. *Notitia* (content or knowledge)

2. *Assensus* (conviction, assent, or intellectual agreement)

3. *Fiducia* (consent, trust, or reliance)

We will just make it easy and refer to these as Content, Conviction, and

Consent. This is Faith.

Content (Notitia)

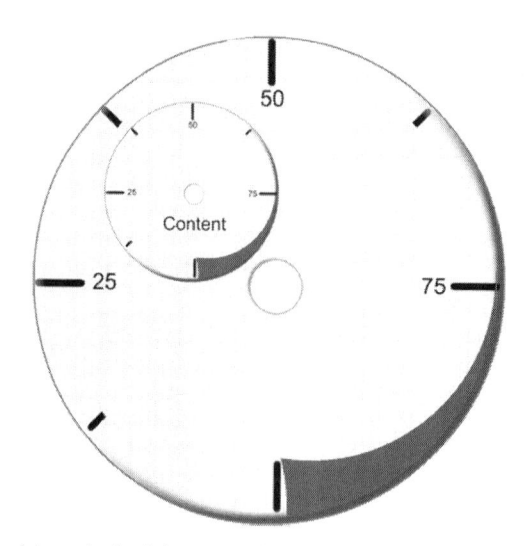

The first of the three sub-meters is the "Content Meter." Most basically, this assumes that knowledge or content is necessary for our faith. There is no such thing as faith without content (we will talk more about that later).

The Reformers referred to this as *notitia*.

This content, or knowledge, consists of propositions, basic historical claims, stories, and ideas. For example, Christians claim that God created the world out of nothing, loves all people, is involved in history, and sent Christ, the God-man, to die for our sins. We also claim that a person's faith in Christ puts them in a right ("saving") relationship with God. Finally, among other things, we claim that the Bible is God's inspired word. Each of these claims is part of the content of our faith.

As much as I hate to say it, content is not really black and white either. Believing that the Bible is God's word does not ensure that people are going to *interpret* it in the same way. Involved in the content meter is an assumption of *correct* understanding. Without this, people may believe, but their belief is based on misinformation, misunderstanding, and/or misinterpretation. This is why it is so important that we not only have the right content, but that we are interpreting the content correctly.

Conviction (Assensus)

Here is the second meter that makes up our overall faith. This is the "Conviction Meter." It expresses the level of *intellectual assent* one has about the content. It asks the question, "Do you *really* believe these things?" As with content, there is no such thing as faith without conviction.

The Reformers called this *assensus*.

The conviction of one's faith depends on how much they have actually wrestled with the content. This assumes that the faith is not blind. It *assumes* that it is not an Indiana Jones-like step of faith. It involves trustworthy resources, rational thinking, and intellectual exploration of opposing ideas. One may have knowledge that Christ rose from the grave, but there is a point where this knowledge turns into a conviction that the proposition is *actually* true. A *complete* absence of conviction is evidence that one's beliefs are not real.

This may seem self-evident, but (as I hope to demonstrate soon) it is not always the case. Some people, like Indiana Jones in his "step of faith," have a type of faith that is greatly lacking in true conviction.

Consent (Fiducia)

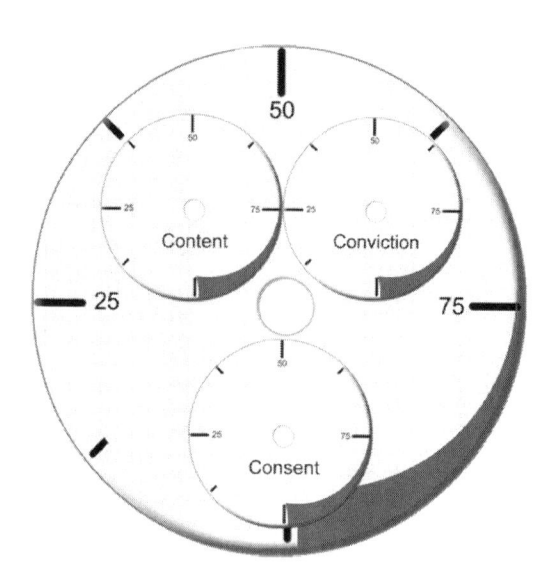

Finally we add the "Consent Meter" to the mix. I must admit that the word "consent" is based more on my desire to alliterate for didactic purposes than on my desire for accuracy, but I think it will work if you follow me.

The idea of consent has to do with the actions our convictions bring about, producing true faith. I think there are two other good words (that don't start with "c") that can be used to express this element just as well: trust and reliance. While the other two aspects of faith were both informative and intellectual, this one involves an act of the will. This is where we *decide* or *concede* to place our faith in the object of our conviction.

While some may think "consent" would be better placed as a synonym for "conviction," I do believe it fits here very nicely, especially for the Christian faith. We are called upon to turn to God in faith. This will frequently mean that we are turning away from something else. It is a *surrender of the will*. We are to concede our lives to God. To concede our lives means that we are no longer self-reliant or self-secure, but are resting or trusting in God. Pride is the opposite of consent. One can have all the right knowledge, and even possess a strong conviction that it is true, but never overcome their pride enough to yield or concede their lives to God.

Perfect Faith

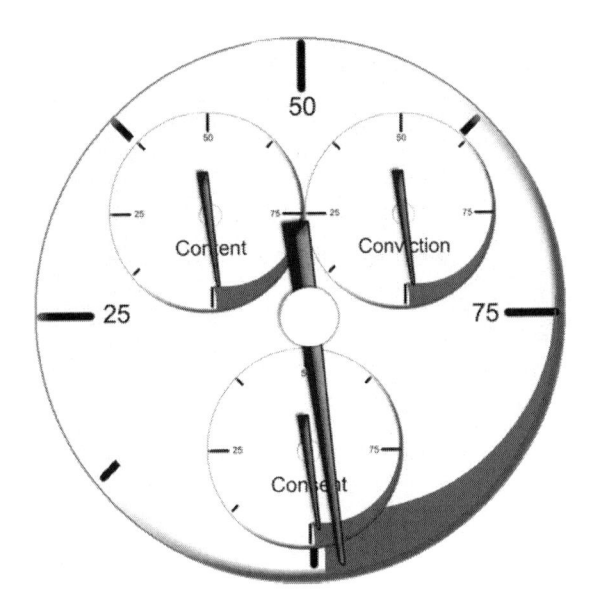

This is a picture of perfect faith. Actually, let me restate that. This is a picture of the perfect faith — *which nobody has, this side of heaven.* We would all like to have all of our meters in the red zone, but none of us do. Even after writing this book, my faith is not perfect. After reading this book, yours will not be perfect either. We should not expect to have perfect faith in this life. All of us have some wrong content, different levels of conviction, and areas of our lives that we have not conceded over to God.

Look at the Belief-O-Meter again. I want you to notice how the three sub-meters are connected to the big one. When the sub-meters rise, the big meter (which, I remind you, represents the whole of your faith) will rise accordingly. We have a fancy name for the process of getting all of these meters to rise: sanctification.

The following chapters will illustrate how our faith rises and falls with each meter.

Discussion questions:

1. Do you agree that no one this side of heaven can have perfect faith? Explain.

2. Describe what consent looks like with no conviction.

3. Of the three meters, which component of faith do you see today's church lacking most? Explain.

4. Of the three meters, which component of faith do you see your church lacking most? Explain.

5. On the overall faith meter, where would you rank your faith right now? Why?

6. Where would you rank yourself on each one of the meters? Which do you need to work on?

Keeping the Big Picture:

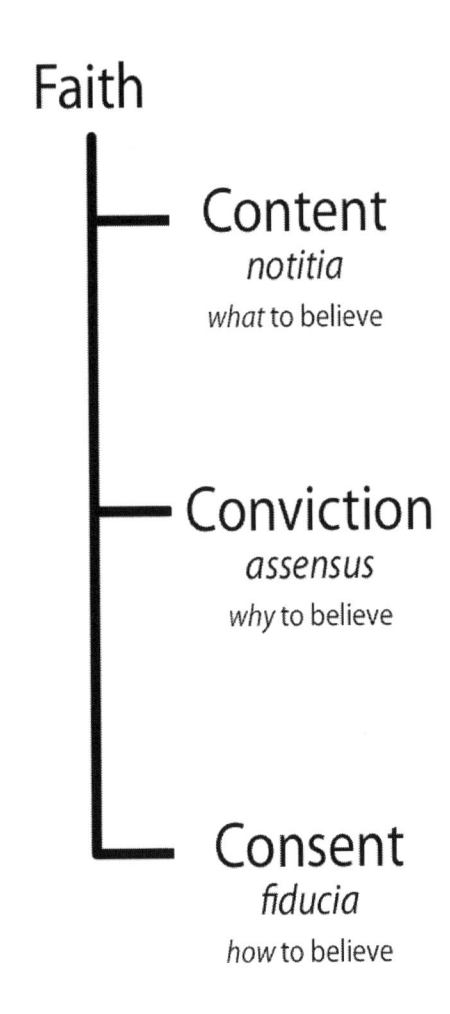

Faith
- **Content**
  notitia
  what to believe

- **Conviction**
  assensus
  why to believe

- **Consent**
  fiducia
  how to believe

CHAPTER #2

KNOWING *WHAT* YOU BELIEVE

Some time ago Evangelical pollster and sociologist George Barna concluded, based on numerous surveys, that nearly 40% of the individuals sitting in the pews of Evangelical Churches do not have enough content to their faith to be saved. Christian Smith, the director of the National Study of Youth and Religion and associate chair of Sociology at the University of North Carolina at Chapel Hill, coined the label "Moralistic Therapeutic Deism" to describe the religion of America's youth in his 2005 book *Soul Searching: The Religious and Spiritual Lives of American Teenagers*. This means the God that today's youth are worshiping is very different from the God of the Bible. In her fascinating book Almost Christian, Kenda Creasy Dean, associate professor of Princeton Theological Seminary, talks about the faith of America's youth. In it, she says that while 75% of today's youth claim the name "Christian," only 8% take their faith seriously. In a chapter provocatively entitled "Mormon Envy," she argues that Mormons are doing a much better job of passing on the content of their faith to their kids. Most Evangelicals, she argues, are satisfied with merely hoping that the content of their faith will someday be assumed by their children. However, Barna's research shows that this is not happening.

CHAPTER 2: KNOWING WHAT YOU BELIEVE

I remember the Peanuts cartoon where Linus is waiting for the Great Pumpkin, who is dreadfully late. I think it was Lucy who attempted to comfort him with the words, "It does not matter what you believe as long as you are sincere."

As well, I recall an AT&T commercial from a few years ago, where people stand in lines in downtown New York City holding up signs that say, "I believe." The next scene shows a high-rise apartment, where a banner hung from a window reads, "I believe." Next, a plane flies by towing a banner which says, "I believe." Finally, a police officer sits on his horse in the middle of the street with a sign, "I believe." Then the AT&T logo came on the screen and the commercial was over. I thought to myself, "You believe *what*?" When I was in Washington, DC, a few months ago, I saw over the window of Macy's their new slogan: "Believe." Believe *what*?

We live in a culture that loves to talk about faith, belief, and spirituality. Unfortunately, we frequently find this belief going to the prom stag. It is not accompanied by any content. More often than not, there is nothing to believe in or to believe *that*. It is just that people *believe* – no object necessary. It is a virtue to be a "believer" so long as you don't know *what* you believe. In fact, if you accompany your belief with an object, your "faith" will quickly become the subject of ridicule and scorn. This is especially the case if the content of your belief necessarily excludes other options. Many think it is best these days to just believe. We call this "postmodernism."

We also live in a time where the basic content of the Christian faith is not being passed on accurately. It is being screened through a filter of political correctness, therapeutic necessity, and seeker sensitivity. It seems we are taking a cue from Burger King, telling people to "have it your way." Have God your way! We call this *American individualism* and *commerce*.

With regard to the Christian faith, a content-less faith is not possible. When the Reformers talked about faith, they understood that faith must be *in* something. It has to have substance. One's faith can only grow to the degree that substantial and definite content is present. Both a lack of content and accuracy can cause one's faith to be seriously troubled.

Postmodern Faith

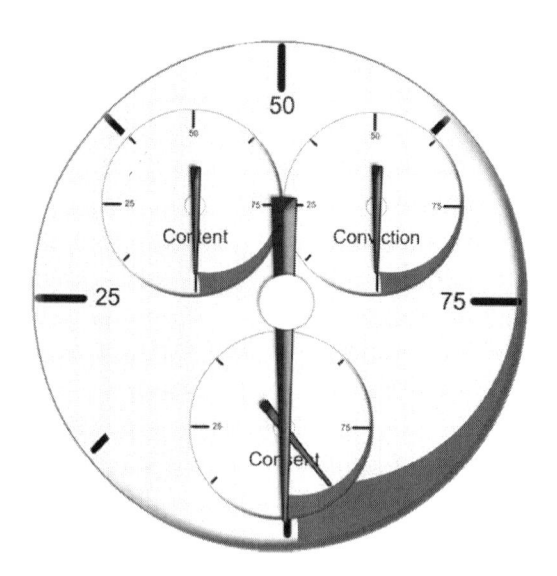

Notice here the "consent" sub-meter. Consent represents the idea of trust. The postmodern mindset is very favorable toward spirituality and belief. Therefore, their consent (trust) meter is theoretically very high. They are people of faith, remember. But due to the confusion that exists with respect to content, they are unwilling to commit themselves to a belief *in* something or belief *that* something. It is a naked belief. There are simply too many options out there, and to commit to one is to condemn the other. Who are we to say that *we* are right and *they* are wrong? Besides all this, there is internal conflict among those who agree. In other words, even those who agree eventually part ways over disagreements. The postmodern looks at Christianity and says, "Which one? Catholic? Orthodox? Baptist? Presbyterian? Methodist? or one of the divisions of these? It is better to be a person of faith, but not choose which faith."

Notice the conviction meter is turned off, since there is no content about which to be convicted. The big meter, which represents the totality of one's faith from a Biblical standpoint, is at zero. No matter how high the consent meter, one's faith is not going to be affected. It is impossible to have faith without any content, no matter what Lucy, AT&T, and Macy's tell you. One cannot be a believer without an object in which to believe.

Yes, this will create divisions. Yes, this will get you labeled with that nasti-

est of titles: intolerant. However, our tolerance or intolerance is not to be decided by committee, culture, family, or individual opinion (even yours), but by God and his revelation. If his introduction of himself causes us to say that other descriptions of him and what he requires are wrong, so be it. We are in the pursuit of truth, not favorable opinions.
Christ said it this way:

Matthew 10:34-39
"Do not suppose that I have come to bring peace to the earth. I did not come to bring peace, but a sword. 35 For I have come to turn " 'a man against his father, a daughter against her mother, a daughter-in-law against her mother-in-law – 36 a man's enemies will be the members of his own household.' 37 "Anyone who loves his father or mother more than me is not worthy of me; anyone who loves his son or daughter more than me is not worthy of me; 38 and anyone who does not take his cross and follow me is not worthy of me. 39 Whoever finds his life will lose it, and whoever loses his life for my sake will find it.

Truth is a sword that will divide. Your beliefs will divide you as well.

Least-Common-Denominator Faith

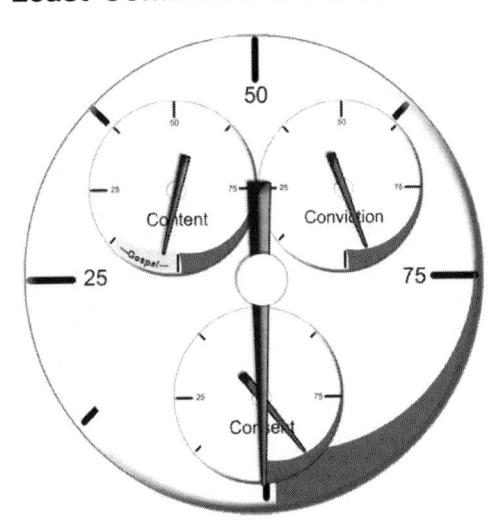

Often, people's solution to the problem of disagreements over content in the church and society is to opt for as little content as possible. This constitutes a "least common denominator" type of faith. Most liberally, this may boil down to a simple belief in a God who is good, loves all people, wants us to do what is right, and has goodies for us in the afterlife. This way all people can make it to heaven. The content, while low, is accompanied by a large degree of conviction and consent. However, as can be seen, this definition of faith does not affect the large meter at all. Why? Because in order for the large meter to begin to move at all (which represents saving faith), there has to be a minimum amount of content present, sufficient to construct the essentials of the Gospel. If the Gospel is absent or grossly distorted, the faith meter cannot budge. In the current graphic, the content meter must move *beyond* the marked "Gospel" area before there is a chance for true biblical faith to exist. This type of faith – belief without the essentials of the Gospel – is what we see in liberal churches all over the world, no matter the denomination.

The components of belief that I would include in the yellow are:

- Belief in God

- Belief that Jesus is God's Son

- Belief that Jesus died on the cross for our sins

- Belief that you are a sinner in desperate need of Christ's redemption

- Belief that Jesus rose from the grave

- Belief that the person is sinful and in need of God's mercy

Essentially, after a belief in God is established, I boil the essentials for salvation (as far as content is concerned) down to the person and work of Christ as defined by historic Christianity.

Shallow Faith

Next, I present to you what I call "shallow faith." Unlike the previous ver-

CHAPTER 2: KNOWING WHAT YOU BELIEVE

sion, we now have a minimal amount of content that is able to issue forth *saving* faith. In other words, the content of their conviction and consent rests in the person and work of Christ. However, notice that the content does not go much further than this. While the conviction is pretty high, it is not as high as the previous example, due to the (still low) amount of content. The more content there is, the harder it is for the conviction to come intuitively. In other words, when content is low, it is easier to have conviction about it since there is not much to be convicted about. When content raises, we have to work more to increase our conviction. The consent (trust) in this example remains very high.

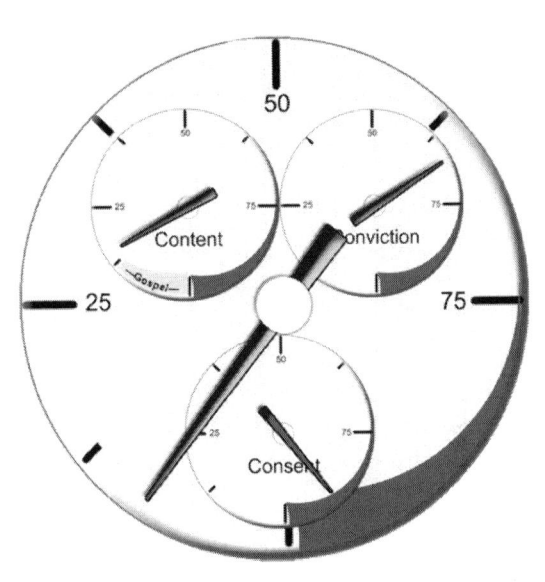

The key thing to notice is that this person's overall faith is still not very strong. The big meter's reading did not increase much. This is due to the lack of content present. People can have a strong trust and conviction in Christ, but remain children in their faith due to lack of information. I believe this is representative of so many in pop-Evangelicalism today. The "tastes great, less filling" mentality of a seeker-centered church, while wonderful in getting people into biblical faith, will not have much success in increasing people's faith beyond that point. I know that not all seeker churches are this way, but I have seen too many that are.

But isn't this enough? We have the person saved, with a good degree of conviction and consent, why burden them with more content than is necessary to bring them into the Kingdom?

The best way to answer this is by way of analogy. Let me try here. Men, suppose you were to approach your wife with this attitude. Just after you get married, your wife seeks to deepen your relationship by getting to know one another.

You respond, "Hold on there. I know enough about you to love you. I don't want or need to know any more."

Your wife says, "Yes, you know many of the main things about me, but I want you to know more."

You respond, "Nope. I know enough. I know your name, height, weight, what you look like, that you are a Republican, that you are a girl, that you love God, and that you love me. That is all I need. I don't want to know about your past, your family, what your high school experience was like, how many kids you want, what kind of music you like, who your best friend is and why, nor do I want to know about your brothers and sisters."

"But," she says, "I have *so* much to tell you."

"No way," you bite back, "there might be something I don't like. Plus, it is hard to sit and listen to all of that. Who knows if I will interpret you correctly anyway. Those things can get confusing. Let me just love you based on these few things and no more."

As you know, this would never work. The relationship would never grow. Eventually, it would go in the wrong direction, leading to disaster. It is the same with God. When we enter into a relationship with him, it is crucial to get to the most important details first. However, there is so much God wants to share with us. He has written a rather large book to inform us about all the things he has done, what he is going to do, and how we can live for him. He has told us about himself in great detail. Yes, a lot of it is confusing and can be discouraging. But there is a lot more to content than just the basics.

The writer of the book of Hebrews put it this way to his readers, who had a very low reading on their content meter:

Hebrews 5:12-14
[B]y this time you ought to be teachers, you need someone to teach you the elementary truths of God's word all over again. You need milk, not solid food! 13 Anyone who lives on milk, being still an infant, is not acquainted with the teaching about righteousness. 14 But solid food is for the mature, who by constant use have trained themselves to distinguish good from evil.

We always need to work towards graduating from the "milk" of our initial knowledge of God to the "meat" of maturity.

In sum, our faith cannot grow much without much content, no matter how sincerely we believe it. This is why it is so important for us, as Christians, to study God's word and God's world. This is why we spend so much time in Bible study and interpretation. This is why we read the *whole* of Scripture, not just the parts we like and are easy to believe. God calls on us to increase our faith, but without continually examining the content that he has given us, we will never be able to do this. Many people are stagnant in their faith, not because of a lack of trust or conviction, but because of the lack of information upon which to base their trust and conviction.

Mormons may be doing a better job of passing on the content of their faith, but it is the wrong content. Content cannot be abandoned. We need to be writing it on the doorposts of our houses and on the collars of our shirt. We need to talk about it as we rise and as we sit. Most importantly, content does not just happen. It has to be taught and it has to be taught often.

It *does* matter *what* you believe; sincerity alone is worth very little.

Discussion Questions:

1. Why do you think the culture is so hesitant to allow content to their faith?

2. Give some examples of what contentless faith looks like.

3. How big of a problem do you think contentless faith is in the church today? Explain.

4. Christ said that he came to divide the world, not unite it. How does Christ divide the world?

5. Why do you think God went to so much trouble to write such an extensive book as the Bible?

6. What are some ideas to strengthen you faith by moving from milk to meat?

Keeping the Big Picture:

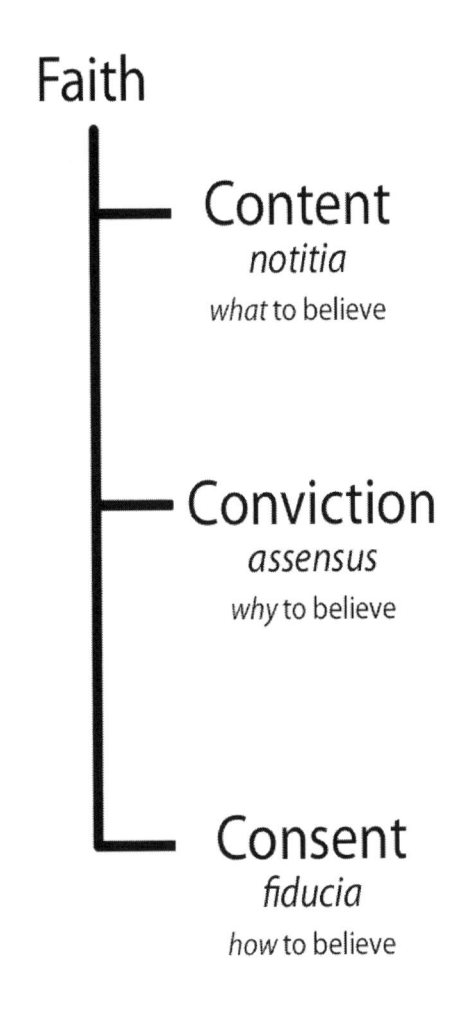

Faith
- # Content
  notitia
  what to believe

- # Conviction
  assensus
  why to believe

- # Consent
  fiducia
  how to believe

CHAPTER #3

KNOW *WHY* YOU BELIEVE

I remember being out one night with a friend in Arizona. I was 20 years old. My friend and I were about the craziest guys in town, with little good reputation to boot. Yet this guy was worse than me. He had a death wish and swore he would not live past 24. But I loved him very much. This particular night, we were bar hopping, looking for trouble. As was typical for me in those days, I would get drunk and start to talk about Jesus. For better or worse, I was ready to lay it on this guy. This night was his night to get saved, if I had anything to say about it. The Holy Spirit would have to work through my slurring. Either way, I was not going to stop until this guy was in the kingdom.

To make a long story short, the guy started the night as an atheist, but he ended the night having "believed" in Christ. Now, don't get too excited, for that is not the direction that this story *really* goes. Let me make a long story just a bit longer. Here is how it all turned out. After many hours of discussion, I kept telling him, "All you have to do is believe that Christ died on the cross for your sins and rose from the dead." He said, "Michael, I don't get it. So you're saying that all I have to do is believe that Christ died for my sins and I will be saved?" "That is it," I responded. "So," he continued, "I don't have to stop drinking or living the way I do?" "No," I said, "It is not about that. It is just about belief. Believe in the Lord Jesus Christ and you will be saved." I could tell that he was a bit confused about this *way* of believing that I was attempting to get him to commit to. It felt like I was trying to get him to sign on the dotted line. "Fine!" he finally responded with an exhausted laugh, "I believe. Now I'm going to heaven. Can we quit talking about it now?" "Yep," I responded with relief, "you are good."

What you can probably see is that there was no true conviction in his confession. He just wanted to get me off his back. But at the same time, I think this minimalistic idea of belief was attractive to him. He was able to "believe" without really believing.

Over the years, nothing changed with this guy, but I wanted to hold on to the idea that he really had an encounter with true Christian belief that day. I simply hoped that it "took." But years later, when we talked about Christ again, there was no conviction and no concession. It had all vanished.

So far we have talked about the three components of faith that must be present for salvation:

1. Content (*Notitia*): knowledge

2. Conviction (*Assensus*): persuasion

3. Consent (*Fiducia*): trust

My friend's "faith" is what content, plus a bit of concession, look like without conviction. True faith cannot be present without *some* degree of real conviction.

Cultural Christian Faith

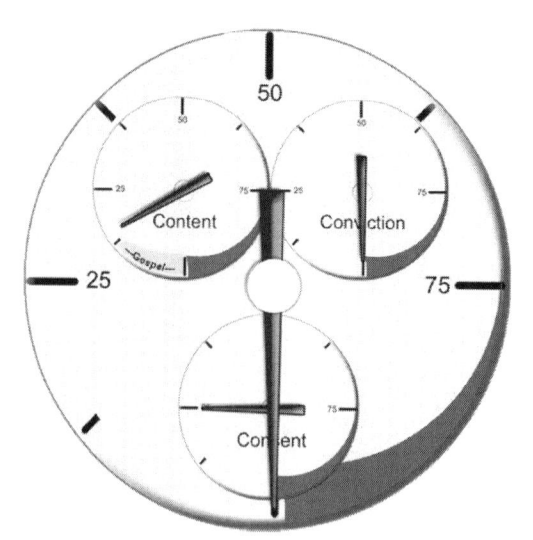

Notice our new meter. Take a long look at it. See that there is sufficient content to produce a Christian faith (it raises above the yellow). Notice as well that the consent is present to *some degree*. However, the big faith meter (representing true faith) is still at zero. Why? Because there is no conviction whatsoever. This type of person is a Christian of convenience.

There are many reasons why someone would possess a faith of convenience or a "cultural" faith, but let me list two common (and related) reasons:

Family Heritage

Many grew up in Christian homes. Mom and dad were Christians, so they are Christian. Mom and dad prayed before meals, so they pray before meals. Mom and dad went to church, so they go to church. This is a sort of "genetic" faith. From very early, many are indoctrinated with the content of Christianity and never question its reality. They simply assume it to be true. This assumption may produce an emotional consent but, more often than not, no conviction is present. Conviction is not passed on from father to son. In other words, faith is not inherited. Conviction is very personal and cannot be indoctrinated. This type of person may never *really* believe all the stuff they "believe" is true, but they think it is "in their blood" nonetheless.

Cultural Habit

For many in the Western world, their faith is a part of the will and testament of their society. They celebrate Christmas because it is a deeply held tradition. They sing Christmas carols because they grew up hearing them. The pathways in their brains have endeared them to everything to do with Christianity, but their faith is nothing more than a habit borne of societal norms. Their confession is a habit. Their prayers are a habit. Even their Bible reading, when present, is a habit.

The most important thing to understand here is that culture and family heritage can produce consent to the basics of Christianity that looks (and often feels) very real, but may not be representative of true faith at all. Without some intellectual conviction, biblical faith is not present. There has to be a time when a person is convinced, at least to some degree, that the basic truths of Christianity are *really* true, not just culturally convenient.

A Pastor without Conviction

I talked to a pastor the other day on the phone. While I will leave his identity anonymous, I will share his story. When I talked to him he was very disturbed. He said that he had been in the pulpit for over 30 years, loved his job, loved preaching, and loved his congregation. "So what's the problem?" I asked him. "I don't know where else to turn," he said. "You seem like a person who will understand without judging." "Go on," I responded. It took him a while, but finally he was able to put together the confession he was almost too scared to make out loud: "I don't think I believe." "You don't think you believe what?" I responded. "All of it," he said. "All of what?" I asked. "Christianity, the Bible, Christ, everything! I have been in the pulpit for thirty years. My dad was a pastor. My granddad was a pastor. It is all I have ever known!" "What happened?" I asked. "I don't know," he said. "It all started a few months ago when someone challenged me about the inspiration of an Old Testament book. It all seemed to make sense. From there I began to question *everything*. Now I don't think I believe anything that I preach at all. And I don't want to lose my faith."

This is what his faith looked like.

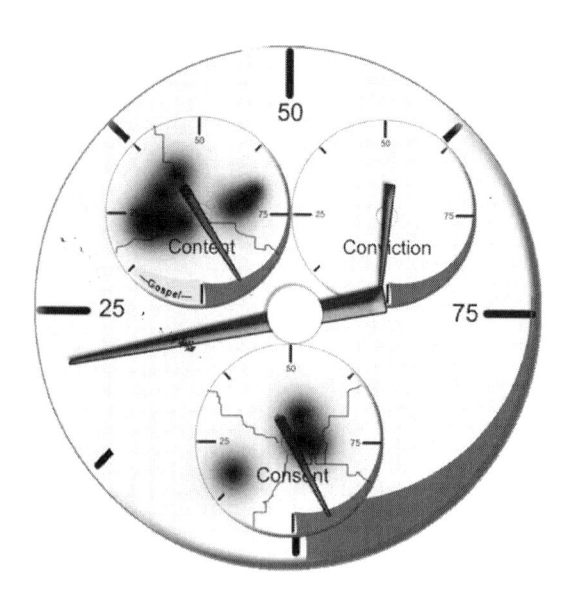

Notice that while the content and consent were very high, they were beginning to fail. Without the aid of conviction, the other two burn out very quickly. When they finally crash, the big meter will go all the way back to zero.

As we talked over the next few weeks, I began to discover that he was never really convinced that Christianity was true. He never took the time to examine his faith and ask, "Is this really true?" so we began examining faith together. I am relieved to say that today, his faith is restored. Through critical examination of those beliefs he took for granted for so many years, he realized they were *really* true. More importantly, his belief is stronger than it has ever been, and so is his preaching!

Blind Faith

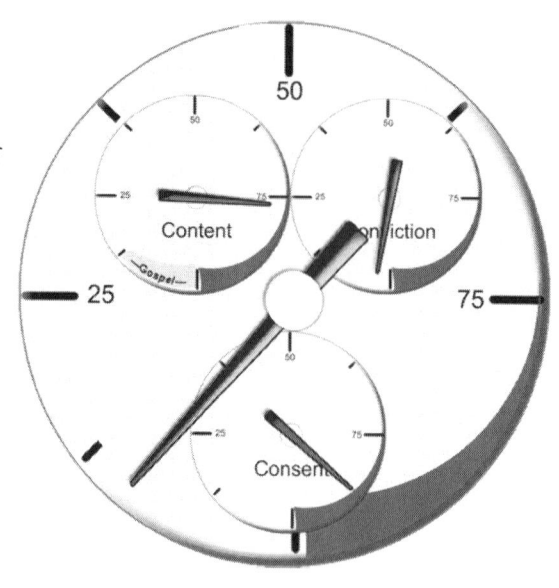

Notice the difference here. We have a *small* amount of conviction brought into the mix. The content is very high with this person's faith. As well, the consent is high. But the main faith meter does not rise too much. Why? Because there is so little conviction.

Many Christians have been indoctrinated with large amounts of content. The word "indoctrination" is often used in a very pejorative way. It normally carries the assumption that there is no critical thinking present. "Oh, you only believe that because you have never allowed yourself to consider alternatives. You are not a FREE thinker." Synonyms for indoctrinate are "brainwash" and "propagandize." Indoctrination is often thought of as the opposite of education, but in reality, it is simply a type of education that discourages critical thinking.

I find this type of faith quite a bit in fundamentalist-type churches. In fact, in many people's minds, critical thinking is an enemy of true faith. To question one's beliefs is anathema (accursed). It is the very antithesis of faith. Some from this ilk actually promote and celebrate blind faith. The blinder the faith, the greater the faith. They completely agree with the scene in *Indiana Jones and the Last Crusade*. Here, there is very little, if any, true examination of alternative options. Growing in faith simply amounts to confirming one's preconceived notions. "Study" and "research" is the process of reviewing your belief by listening to and reading others who already agree with you.

Interestingly, this type of faith *can* produce the most dogmatic and unpleasant believers. By dogmatic, I don't mean informed and legitimately confident. I mean emotional. Those who have little or no intellectual conviction, but a lot of content and consent, often have a very pronounced closet insecurity. This insecurity will sometimes surface when their faith is challenged. Since they don't have any valid reasons for their faith, they resort to emotional defenses, which are fueled by dogmatic methodology. These emotional defenses usually show themselves, not through well-argued and informed responses, but through belittling and shallow attacks on those who hold to alternative beliefs. Their insecurity is often seen in the extreme rhetoric they utilize. All who don't agree with them are heretical, godless, hell-bound, Satan-blinded pagans. To these, *everything* is black and white, true or false, right or wrong. Why? Because without critical engagement, there is no reason to clutter your faith with pesky and confusing uncertainty. You either believe or you don't. To these, it is that simple.

Those who possess this type of faith are normally blind to their own insecurity. Mistaking emotional commitment for intellectual conviction is a very dangerous thing, but this is exactly what happens here. And this is not *just* a characteristic of fundamentalist Christians. It is the same in any faith. In fact, most (but not all) atheists I meet have more blind, uncritical faith than anyone else. They have very little true intellectual engagement of the issues, but a lot of emotion, which drives them to demean anyone who believes in God. Ironically, their main accusation towards those who believe in God is that they are not thinking critically, yet they fail to realize that they are just fundamentalist atheists.

Faith without conviction. Blind faith. Baseless faith. Fundamentalist faith. Cultural faith. Family faith. All of these share the same characteristic: they have no *true* conviction. This is the type of faith to which I brought my friend at the bar. He had no conviction that Christianity was true, and I gave him no reason to think he should. I just wanted him to take a leap of faith. I just wanted him to make the commitment without *really* believing in that to which he was committing. I promoted a blind faith, which was devoid of any value and could not save.

There must be a point where true intellectual engagement happens. The maturation of our faith cannot happen without it. The you-ask-me-how-I-know-he-lives-he-lives-within-my-heart type faith, while it sounds nice, is not a Christian type faith and we should never promote it. Yes, it is much easier to get people to sign on the dotted line when we minimize what faith is, assigning it to mere consent to content, but this is not the faith we are called to.

You must ask yourself if you *really* believe that it is true. Your conviction does not have to be perfect (no one's is), but it does need to be present. Next, I will examine this issue of intellectual conviction by adding three

CHAPTER 3: KNOW WHY YOU BELIEVE

sub-meters to the conviction meter: *certitudo*, *firmitas*, and *evidentia*. Yes, I am going to complicate things a bit more. For this, I am sorry, but in order for us to examine our own faith, we must pull out the Exacto knife, so we can have some clarity. My hope is that this will serve you in building your own conviction.

Discussion Questions:

1. Do you see the church today promoting this "sign on the dotted line" approach to faith? Explain.

2. If faith is reduced to mere emotional consent, what problems may arise in the future?

3. Read Matthew 22:34. How does this verse relate to the subject of this chapter?

4. What areas of your faith lack intellectual conviction? How can you change this?

5. The book of Acts says that after Christ rose from the grave he stayed on the earth for many days giving "many convincing proofs" of his resurrection. How does this support the idea that God does not want us to have "blind faith"?

Keeping the Big Picture:

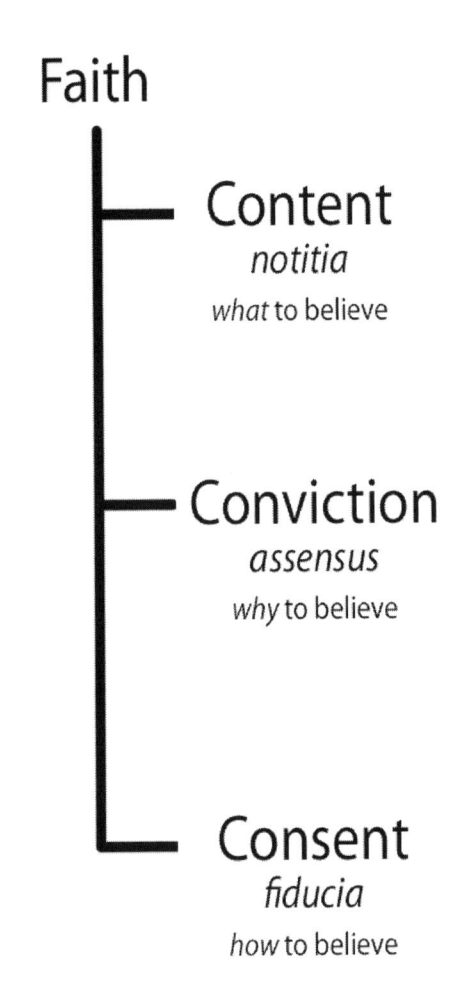

Faith
- **Content**
  notitia
  what to believe

- **Conviction**
  assensus
  why to believe

- **Consent**
  fiducia
  how to believe

CHAPTER #4

CONVICTION

I often tell people that when they are speaking, there are a few ways to sound more authoritative in the eyes of your listeners. First, speak more loudly. If that does not work, speak more deeply. And if both of those don't work, speak with a British accent! Now, though, I am going to give you some insider information by telling you two more ways to convince others to acknowledge your authority. Mind you, these two tips only work with Protestants. First, include the phrase, "the Reformers taught this same thing." If you want to get really fancy, designate them as the *magisterial scholastic* Reformers. Although most Protestants have no clue who the magisterial scholastic Reformers are, it does not matter. It will work. Second (warning: only use this with *extreme* caution and don't try this alone), when you *really* want people to bow to your authority, throw in a Latin word here and there. If you combine all of these, people will be helpless to avoid falling under your spell. The audience is yours.

Already in this book I have employed the two "insider" techniques mentioned above. The magisterial scholastic Reformers talked about three aspects of true Christian faith: 1) *notitia* – content or knowledge, 2) *assensus* – conviction or intellectual assent, and 3) *fiducia* –

CHAPTER 4: CONVICTION

consent, rest, or trust. Now let me expand upon the *assensus* just a bit.

We are talking about the anatomy of faith and all its complexities. Because of this, we must be diligent to discuss all of its intricacies. When it comes to the idea of conviction that we began examining in the last chapter, we must realize there are different types of, and sources for, our conviction. When we ask someone (including ourselves) why we believe what we believe, we must be prepared for a variety of answers. Sometimes these answers will be valid and sometimes they will be invalid.

The Bible tells us to always be ready to give a reason for the hope that lies within us (1Pet. 3:15). If someone asked you, "Why are you a Christian?" what would you say? Take a minute to think about this.

Here are some typical responses:

Why are you a Christian, John? "Because it makes the most sense out of the world."

Why do you believe in God, Emily? "Because I have experienced his love."

Why do you believe the Bible is inspired, Nate? "Because of fulfilled prophecy."

Why do you believe Christ is coming again, Carrie? "Because he said he would and I trust him to do what he says."

How do you know the Bible has been accurately handed down, Tim? "Because Dr. Daniel B. Wallace has studied the manuscript evidence and come to the conclusion that it is trustworthy."

The convictions expressed by each answer here are based on different criteria. The scholastic magisterial Reformers (!) said there are three types of conviction which make up one's overall assent to their faith. I am going to use my own terms here to keep things simple (and because we already know

I am a fan of alliteration).

Take a look at our Belief-O-Meter. We are going to be adding some sub-meters to the conviction meter. Conviction is made up of all three sub-elements. The more of each sub-element present, the greater one's conviction.

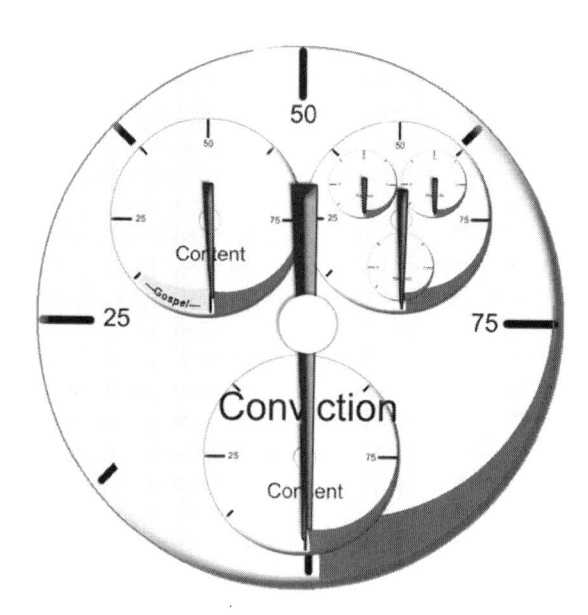

Rational Conviction (What the Reformers called evidentia):

Rational conviction comes by means of intuitive logic. It can be described most simply as sound judgment, common sense, perception, and that which is agreeable to sound reasoning. In some ways, it's the stuff you just figure out. In a more technical sense, it describes the foundational principles of logic which, when used correctly, produce reliable inferences. This involves the law of non-contradiction (A ≠ -A at the same time and in the same relationship). For example, I cannot be wearing shoes and not wearing shoes when both propositions assume the same time frame and the same definition for "shoes." "Duh!" you say. "Exactly!" I say. It is intuitive. It is common sense.

This is a very important aspect of our conviction. We want to have faith that makes sense and does not fly in the face of other things that we know to be true. When something is not rational, we call it irrational. An irrational faith is a faith that will be necessarily void of much true conviction. Why? Because we believe that God has created us as rational beings, mirroring his own rational character. In other words, our beliefs cannot be illogical or

CHAPTER 4: CONVICTION

formally absurd. Confusing? Yes. Paradoxical? You bet. Mysterious? Often. Violating the rules of logic? No.

The question here is this: Does your faith do justice to rational thinking or does it violate it?

Real Life Conviction (What the Reformers also called evidentia):

The second is real life conviction. This most broadly refers to human experience. It is often called "empirical," meaning that which we observe or experience with our senses – it is stuff we can see, feel, taste, touch, or test. It has to do with evidence. This can come by way of direct personal encounters or by historical verification. Whereas rational conviction comes intuitively and works primarily off of logical deduction, real life conviction comes by way of subjective encounter, evidence, and testing.

The Apostles believed that Christ rose from the grave not because of intuitive necessity (e.g., God, by definition, must rise from graves), but because of firsthand experience. They saw Christ die and then rise from the grave. Many believe that the Bible is reliable because they have studied it and compared it to historical verification (e.g., internal evidence, external evidence) and their own lives (e.g., the Bible says I am a sinner and I have experienced sin). This would be real life conviction. It is based on the accumulation of various types of evidence.

The question here is this: Is there any *evidence* to support your faith claims, or are they based only on subjective opinion?

Referred Conviction (what the Reformers called *firmitas* and *certitudo*)

Referred conviction is the assurance that you have which is not intuitively nor experientially your own, but from another source. Before you get too down on this one, I think it is important to know that the majority of things you believe are based on referred conviction. This doesn't make it wrong or naive. In fact, the smartest people in the world have beliefs that are primarily dependent on another's conclusions. The question is not whether or not you are going to have referred conviction, but how reliable your sources are.

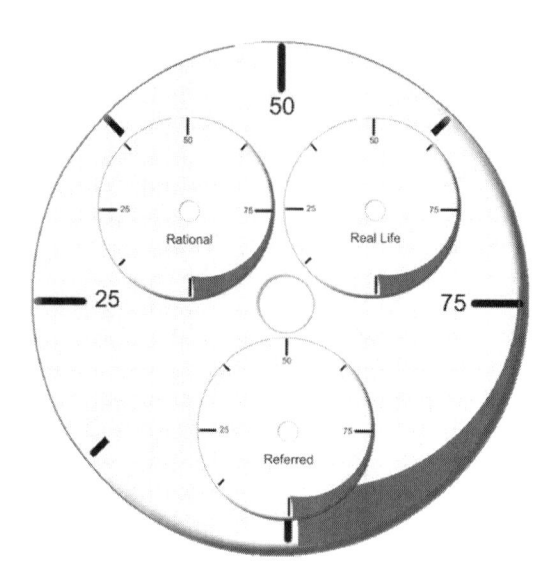

Most people start with referred conviction based on what mom and dad taught them. With little ability to be rationally critical and very little experience to draw from, a child's conviction meter is going to be based on what others have told them. If they trust their parents (which most children do), then they will be convicted of the same things about which their parents are convicted.

However, if most people are honest, they will realize that referred conviction is not *necessarily* a black eye to their beliefs. Nor would we suppose that all areas of our belief must eventually be personally attained. I, for example, believe in the existence of Mt. Everest. I think my conviction is pretty stable and secure. However, I have never actually seen Mt. Everest (that I can remember). Neither could I pick it out of a photo lineup right now. I don't even know what it looks like. However, I remain secure in my

CHAPTER 4: CONVICTION

belief due to the reliability of referred conviction. This often comes by way of common public knowledge and acceptance, but also by way of reliance on one or two trusted sources. I have never dated the New Testament manuscript called P52 (John Rylands Papyrus). I would not be very good at dating it. However, there are scholars who know what they are doing who date it to around AD 125. I trust them because I am familiar enough with the field and with these scholars' reputations to justify referred conviction in this situation.

In other words, it is okay to stand on the shoulders of another person's conviction. What we must not do is *blindly* stand on the shoulders of another person's conviction. We will get back to this later.

Conviction is very complex, yet it can also be very simple. When it comes to our faith, we need to have strong conviction that it is true. We must engage the intellect. We must be willing to change according to the evidence. We must have trustworthy sources to which we refer. As we will see, though, there are many who will neglect one or more of these aspects causing their conviction to be seriously weakened. As I have been arguing, a weak intellectual conviction is ultimately going to produce weak faith.

Next I will break down each one of these and show what faith looks like without rational, real life, or referred conviction.

Discussion Questions:

1. If someone were to ask you why you are a Christian, what would you say?

2. Give some example about how a belief in the existence of God is rational.

3. What are some examples of experiences (real-life conviction) you have had that strengthen your faith?

4. What are some areas in your life where you have to refer on the knowledge or expertise of another? Are you confident in your reliance on them? Why or why not.

5. It was said that our faith will never be irrational because rationality is from the very essence of God. If our faith could be irrational, this would mean that God can act and reveal himself in ways that are against his character. His character is rational, but he can act irrationally? His character is truthful, but he can lie? What would such an idea (God can act and reveal himself in ways that do not line up with who he is) do to the Christian faith? Explain.

Keeping the Big Picture:

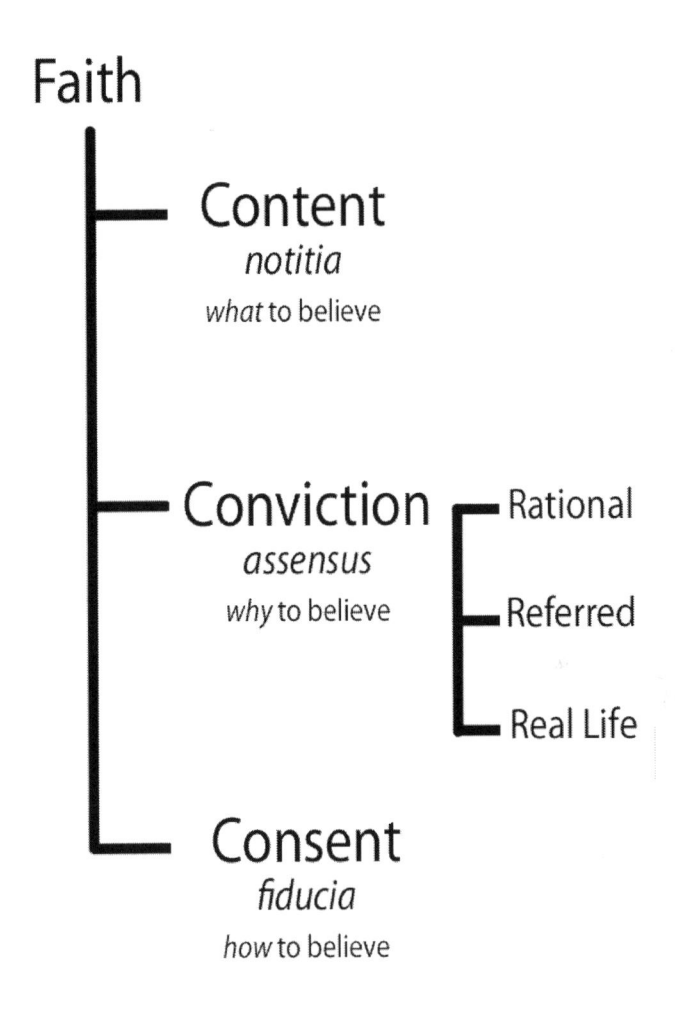

Faith
- **Content**
  notitia
  what to believe

- **Conviction**
  assensus
  why to believe
  - Rational
  - Referred
  - Real Life

- **Consent**
  fiducia
  how to believe

CHAPTER #5

REFERRED CONVICTION

There are so many things I don't know about. Yes, I have a master's degree in theology from a four-year program. A master's degree! Yes, my studies were very in depth. And yes, since I graduated almost a decade ago, I have kept up my studies very intently. But I feel like I know less today than I did when I first began. It is often said that a pastor has to be an expert in more areas than any other profession. He has to know history, psychology, grammar, leadership, biology, geography, archeology, hermeneutics, Greek, Hebrew, English, literature, logic, cosmology, rhetoric, paleology, sociology, ethics, marriage, substance abuse, and, yes, even politics. Actually, the more accurate statement would be that a pastor is *perceived by many* to be an expert in more areas than any other field. Sometimes this perception goes to our head and we begin to think of ourselves as masters of all areas. This is *far* from true.

In every area listed, I am but a novice. In many of them, I am just knowledgeable enough to be dangerous. Most people, if they are honest, are *masters* of very few (if any) things (no matter how many degrees they hold). In just about every area of life, we rely heavily on the expertise of others.

CHAPTER 5: REFERRED CONVICTION

Think about this. When you read your Bible, I bet you don't personally translate every passage from the original Greek or Hebrew. You rely on the translation of others. Your confidence in this translation comes from what I have called "referred conviction." You simply trust the people who translated it. For the few that do translate the Bible yourself, my bet is that you don't use a self-constructed Greek or Hebrew text. You probably use a "critical text" that came by way of another's expertise. My point is that no matter how you slice it, you are standing on the shoulders of others and your position is only as stable as those who are holding you up.

We need to be careful about getting too high on ourselves. In our individualistic, "maverick" society, we value individualism. But knowledge, understanding, and wisdom are not individualistic. *No one* is really *that* smart. Most of us are filled with referred intelligence and conviction.

Referred Conviction

Thus far, we have argued that faith is made up of three primary things: content, conviction, and consent. Right now we are zeroing in on conviction. Conviction, as we have defined it, is the intellectual aspect of our faith. This conviction is made up of three things: rationale, real-life experience, and knowledge that has been referred. Our conviction sub-meter looks like this:

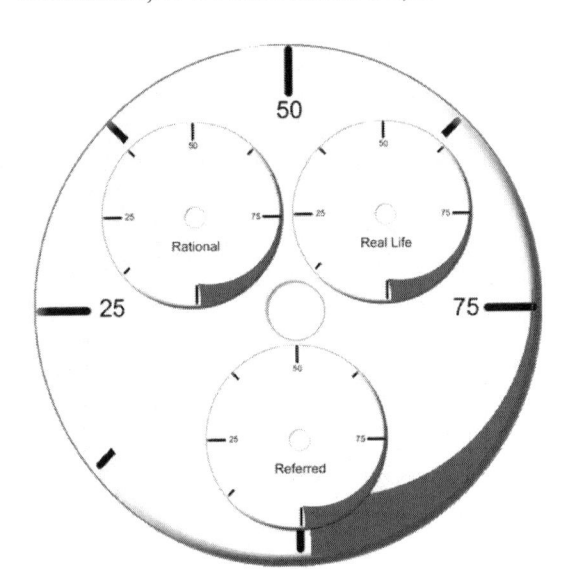

Let's spend some time on "referred conviction." The Reformers called it *firmitas*.

Our faith is going to consist largely of understanding and conviction that relies on other people. I am convinced that 99.9% of the world's information is beyond my ability to have "expert" knowledge of it, much less a firsthand conviction about. There are not too many areas in which I can be an expert. But there are experts out there, both contemporary and historical. There *are* reliable sources to be found. There are reliable people to be read or heard. In fact, Christians believe that finding reliable access to the *ultimate* source for referred conviction is ideal. This ultimate source, as revealed in Scripture, is Jesus Christ. We will expand on this more later. For now, we have to realize that in order to get to the ultimate source of reliable conviction, Jesus Christ, we often have to lean on others.

My library is filled with books written by sources I trust. From New Testament background commentaries to histories of the Reformation, I have to rely on the research of others in my own research. The closest I have ever come to contributing to one of these areas with an original study was when I did some graduate work in the Oxyrhynchus Papyri. What the heck is that? I am glad you asked! The Oxyrhynchus Papyri is a large group of manuscripts dating from the first through fourth centuries. It came from a trash dump filled with letters, receipts, and other documents, found in Egypt in the 1940s. My research goals were to 1) study the characteristics of an amanuensis (scribal secretary) in the first century (how much liberty did they have in their style?) and 2) learn how they used the Greek word *huper* ("for," "on behalf of," or "instead of"). I was trying to correlate this with the use of *huper* in explanations of the doctrine of substitutionary atonement (Rom. 5:6, "Christ died huper [on behalf of] the ungodly"). While my research was incredibly interesting, and I can speak with a good degree of personal authority and conviction on *this* particular topic, it is so narrow that I rarely get any chance (much less find the need) to share my knowledge with others.

Again, no matter your field of study, no matter your IQ, the point is not whether you stand on the shoulders of others; it is whether or not those shoulders are trustworthy. We should not refer our conviction *blindly* to anyone, but we do have to concede that we need others. Knowledge is a community thing. Therefore, conviction is ultimately going to involve community.

CHAPTER 5: REFERRED CONVICTION

Two Sources of Referred Conviction:

(I refuse to create any more sub-meters here, though I could! You can thank me later.)

1. Contemporary Referred Conviction

Contemporary referred conviction comes by way of contemporary testimony. This testimony is provided by those with whom we have some degree of contact, either through extension (books, articles, lectures, podcasts, blogs, and other resources) or through personal engagement (parents, friends, professors, pastors, etc.). They are our contemporaries.

2. Historically Referred Conviction

Historically referred conviction comes by way of historical testimony, which comes from those who have gone before us. For Christians, we believe we are members the Body of Christ. We believe that each Christian contributes in some way to this body. What many are unaware of (especially in Protestantism) is that the Body of Christ is made up of those who are both alive and dead. We call this the *communio sanctorum*, or the "communion of saints." We still stand on the shoulders of those who have gone before us. Augustine, Anselm, Aquinas, Luther, Edwards, Lewis, and a thousand others who are all gone, but are all still card-carrying, contributing members to the Body of Christ. Therefore, they are resources for our referred conviction.

As with everything, there are ways in which we can go wrong. Let me expand on a couple.

Arrogant Conviction

Notice here that while both rational and real life (evidence) conviction meters are high, there is no referred conviction present. Hence, the overall conviction meter does not rise much.

Arrogance is defined as the display of superiority and self-pride. The arrogant person thinks too highly of *his own* thoughts and convictions. What they say and believe is right, *no matter what others think*. Proverbs says, "The way of the fool is right in his own eyes" (Prov. 12:15). We need to be careful here, since some of the greatest revolutions in history have come about because certain individuals rightly went against the grain of their culture. Think of Athanasius, Martin Luther, Martin Luther King, Jr., William Wilberforce, and even Jesus himself. Where would we be without them? However, they were not truly mavericks, since they only went against the grain of *contemporary* society. All of them appealed to a *common* good, *common* sense, and had historical referrals under their belt.

The type of person I am talking about has little or no concern for what *anyone* else, contemporary or historical, has to say. Their conviction is based only on their *own* ingenuity. They don't have any desire to ask for help from others. I have seen many Christians who study their faith in such a way. They don't need commentaries, books, or advice, and they certainly don't need to consult history. They and the Holy Spirit have it all figured out. There is no such thing as the *communio sanctorum* for them.

It gets really bad when these people start churches and call on others to join them in their supposed "new" understanding. They are, more often than not, oppressive and authoritative. They hardly encourage their congregants to seek outside guidance. Wisdom comes only when people are bowing to them. Their thoughts and convictions come from no other authority

CHAPTER 5: REFERRED CONVICTION

than themselves. We have a fancy name for this type of person: cultist. They start cults.

Worse yet, many of them will claim this is the essence of the Reformers' ideal of *sola Scriptura* ("the Scripture alone"). "Me, myself, the Holy Spirit, and the Scriptures," they will say. "That is all I need. I have no other authority or reference. My conviction is my own. My interpretation is my own. If it differs from everyone else, living or dead, I am not concerned." But the Reformers did not mean that the Scripture is our *only* source of authority or that private interpretation was ideal; rather, they meant the Scripture is the *ultimate* source of authority and that we need to have our own conviction (understanding that this conviction needs to be informed by historic and contemporary sources).

Outsourced Conviction

What do you notice here? Look closely. Rational and real life experience (evidence) are completely absent. Referred conviction is very high, yet having referred conviction near one hundred still does not move the overall conviction meter very much. Why? Because there has to be balance.

We can only rely exclusively on referred conviction for so long. Of course it is this way when we are children. We refer to mom and dad's beliefs. However, there comes a time when we need to graduate from the beliefs of our parents, pastor, denomination, tradition, and culture. Unfortunately, some people never do. *Every* conviction they have is simply referred conviction from other sources. I call this "outsourced conviction." Sometimes these sources are good, sometimes they are not so good. This type of person neither questions their sources nor puts them to the test. Their conviction is in no way their own.

I find this quite a bit in belief systems that attempt to keep their adherents from "free thinking." These systems discourage asking questions or expressing doubts. Fear is the motivator that keeps their people in check. I just finished counseling a couple whose lives were devastated from years of sitting under an authoritative pastor who threatened them with horrible things (including the loss of their salvation) if they ever sought truth anywhere else. They finally left the church, but still live in fear of his wrath. This is what blindly outsourcing your beliefs can do.

Normally, when this is present in Church, personal Bible study is discouraged. "Just let us take care of that for you," they say. "We are the professionals. If you start to think, you will only mess things up."

This type of methodology does keep things tighter. It does ensure a certain type of unity. And it does recognize the importance of referred conviction. But, in the end, this is what the sixteenth century Reformers rebelled against. It is *the* problem the Reformers reformed! The institutionalized church of the day required that people refer *all* of their beliefs to them. The tragedy produced then is the same as what is produced today: no one has *real* conviction. And remember what happens to your overall belief meter when personal conviction is this low? It just can't get very high.

If we want our faith to be strong, we must have balance. We need to assess whether we are relying too heavily on untested sources or if we are going maverick. We must acknowledge that there is no way to have accurate convictions without leaning on the conviction of others, to a large degree. Those who don't lean on others are denying the presence and power of the Holy Spirit. Proverbs says, "The way of the fool is right in his own eyes." However, Proverbs also teaches, "But a wise man is he who listens to counsel" (Pro 12:15). We must spend our lives working to find trustworthy

CHAPTER 5: REFERRED CONVICTION 57

resources, surrounding ourselves with wise advisers and friends in *every* area.

There are so many things you and I don't know much about. This does not mean our convictions concerning these things have to be ill-founded. Seek humble, reliable, well-studied sources. Stay away from authoritative know-it-alls.

Discussion Questions:

1. Do you have people in your life that you trust and can refer to in specific areas of belief? Who? Explain.

2. Are there great saints of the past that you lean on in specific areas of belief? Who? Explain.

3. Describe a church that does not listen to the voices of the past at all?

4. Describe conviction that is based only on the conviction of others?

5. Is this referred conviction meter high or low for your faith? Please explain.

CHAPTER 5: REFERRED CONVICTION

Keeping the Big Picture:

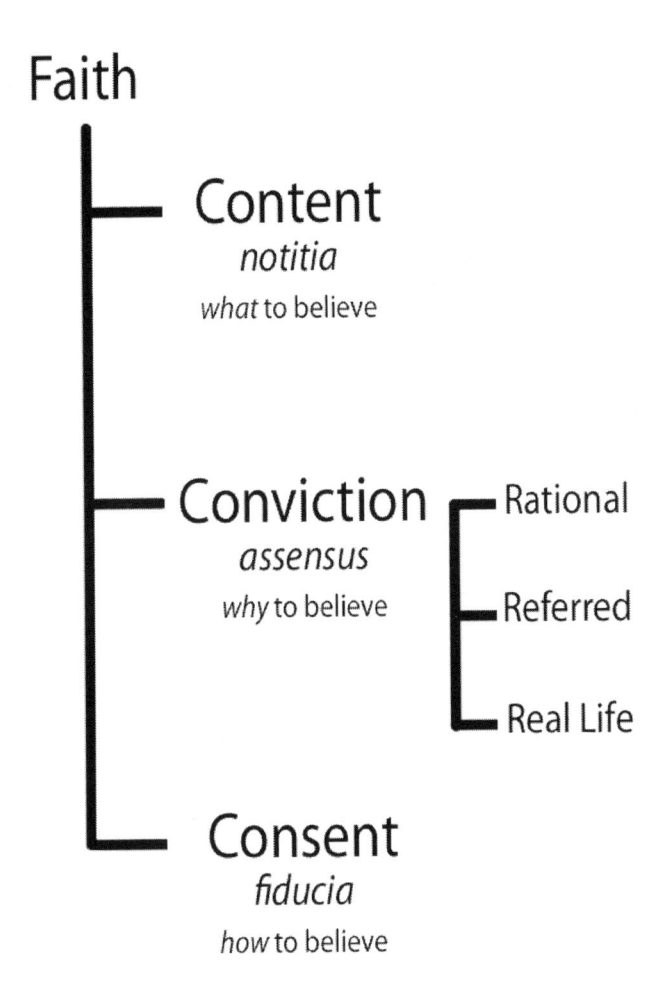

Faith
- **Content**
  notitia
  what to believe
- **Conviction** — Rational
  assensus   — Referred
  why to believe   — Real Life
- **Consent**
  fiducia
  how to believe

CHAPTER #6

RATIONAL CONVICTION

I have done some irrational things in my life. There are way too many to count, but two stand out.

One time, when I was 12 years old, I was riding my Yamaha YZ-80 dirt bike in an undeveloped part of our neighborhood. It was getting dark and rain was starting to fall. There was an 18 foot hill I had been climbing for the last few hours. It had a lip at the top, which was great for jumping. When I saw the rain start to fall and realized it was nearly time to go home, I wanted to get in one last bit of fun. So, I backed away from the hill about forty yards and prepared for my final jump of the day. Normally I would hit the hill at about one-third throttle in second gear. When I got to the top, where the lip was, I would do as any good motocross rider would and give it a slight bit more gas to steady my bike through the jump. However, this time I let go of all good sense. To this day I don't know why, but I gunned it from the beginning and hit third gear full-throttle. By the time I hit the lip, I was flying and had no throttle left to steady the jump. Sure enough, the bike went flying through the air as my body parted from the seat and my hands from the grips. Flying sans bike about fifteen to twenty feet in the air is the last thing I remember.

CHAPTER 6: RATIONAL CONVICTION

About twenty minutes later I woke up on the ground, flat on my face, with my bike twenty feet away from me. I stood up and came to, walked to my bike, and tried to pick it up. It was only then that I noticed the excruciating pain radiating from my shoulder. My clavicle was broken. I stood there and cried until a nice lady stopped and came to my aid.

The other incident happened when I was four years old. Most people remember very little about events from such a young age, but this act of stupidity made a lasting impression on me. We had a dog named Scamper. He was a little Schnauzer who could not have weighed more than eight pounds. I was looking over the second-story balcony of our house when I had a bright idea. I thought I would check to see if Scamper could fly, so I picked him up and dropped him on the hardwood floor twelve feet below. As I stood there looking over the rail at Scamper's motionless body, I knew right away that I had done something wrong. Thankfully, Scamper lived.

In both cases I remember my dad asking me what I used for a brain. In both cases, I failed to use common sense. Neither I nor Scamper could fly.

Rational thinking can be defined as the innate human capacity for reasonable, critical, and analytical mental processes. My dad would just call it common sense. It is "common" because it (allegedly) comes standard with every human brain, no upgrades necessary.

However, many of us choose not to use rational thinking when it comes to God. We often take the Indiana Jones "leap of faith," believing the irrational will somehow be true, bridges we can't see will be there, and dogs really can fly. It is said that the lottery is a tax upon stupid people. This is probably the case. I know individuals who spend their money every day to buy tickets for a lottery they have a less than one in a million chance of winning. However, like me with Scamper, many times people trust in the most unlikely of outcomes, believing that their blind and irrational faith will defy the rules of logic just for them.

It is very hard to justify conviction without rationale.

Rational Conviction

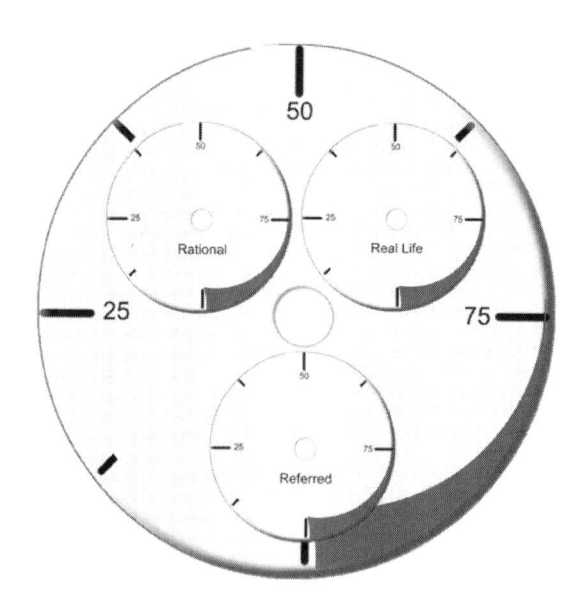

Remember, faith is made up of three essential components: content, conviction, and consent. We are focusing here on conviction, which has three components as well: rational, real life (evidential), and referred conviction.

Our desire is to have all three meters as high as we can, in order for the intellectual conviction of our faith to be secure.

Rational thinking is what the Reformers called *certitudo*. It is something we are born with. Of course, as is assumed here, it is not something that we *must* use. We can be irrational. We *can* believe and do things that don't make a lick of sense.

The Christian faith is a rational faith. Let me repeat that: The Christian faith is a rational faith. Our faith *requires* us to use our minds. How do we know this? Good question. We believe Christianity is rational because we believe rationality is an attribute of God. Being created in the image of God means we too have the ability *and* responsibility to have a rational faith. However, I have come across many people who see rational thinking as the enemy of true spirituality. They believe that using our minds for logical thinking is like kryptonite for a true believer. This attitude is where we get the phrase "blind faith."

Blind faith is irrational faith. This way of thinking has an interesting past. Let's enter into a brief history lesson here. Hang with me for a moment.

CHAPTER 6: RATIONAL CONVICTION

One of the most influential figures in history who helped give rise to the idea that faith must be blind was a seventeenth-century philosopher named Immanuel Kant. Kant was an epistemologist. Epistemology is the study of the theory of knowledge. It describes *how* we know things. Before we talk any more about Kant, I need to tell you about another philosopher that came before Kant. His name was Rene Descartes. He was an overly optimistic philosopher, believing we could be *absolutely* certain about *everything* if we followed the right method of inquiry. Conversely, there was David Hume. He was an overly pessimistic philosopher who believed that we could not be certain of *anything*, given our finitude of understanding. Descartes and Hume were at odds. One thought we could be certain about everything, while the other thought we could be certain about nothing. In comes Immanuel Kant. He hoped to rescue knowledge from both extremes. Therefore, he relegated all knowledge into two categories: the real world, which can be known and understood through observation (what he called the *phenomenal*); and that which cannot be known because it is unknowable (what he called the *noumenal*). Religion, and all matters concerning the knowledge of God and metaphysics, he placed in the *noumenal* category. Kant basically said you can believe in God, but you cannot believe in him like you believe in your friends, your car, or your popcorn machine. However, when you believe in God, you must understand that your belief is not based in knowledge and intellectual conviction, but in blind faith. Therefore, the types of certainty were divided. There were things about which you could be rationally certain (popcorn machines), and things about which you could be religiously certain (God). There were things that you could *really* know, and then there were the rest, which took faith.

Unfortunately, the church bought into Kantian philosophy and has been plagued by it for the last 200 years. From Kant came the now-popular dichotomy between faith and reason. From this dichotomy comes the anti-rationalism so prevalent in the church today. From this comes the unbiblical banishing of *assensus* from the Christian faith.

We have a song to commemorate this. You know, the one that says, "You ask me how I know he lives; he lives within my heart." In other words, I don't have any *true* rationale for my faith; therefore, I appeal to emotional conviction and say it is from the Holy Spirit. Indeed, it could be from the Holy Spirit, but it could just as well be self-produced or from a demon. How do you know the difference?

Many in the evangelical church today have the right information (*notitia*), but they blindly trust in that information without considering it in a rational manner. This is not the way God created us to believe. If you have banished rational thinking from your faith, your true conviction is going to suffer tremendously.

Rational thinking comes by measuring how closely our beliefs correspond to reality and the way things actually work. Having faith that a dog can fly is blind and irrational. Having faith in the lottery is blind and irrational. Having faith that I can gun my throttle in third gear up a twenty-foot hill is, well, just plain stupid.

"But, God is above logic. He transcends logic. Therefore, to believe in him is to transcend logic."

Or, more technically:

"Our understanding says "A." But God transcends our understanding. Therefore in God's world "A" can equal "non-A." Therefore, believing in "non-A" is godly faith exercised."

A certain theologian once said that Christian wisdom is the act of embracing both sides of a contradiction. While this sounds nice and profound (and, sadly, gains quite an audience), think of the implications. It is really no different than what the snake said to Eve in the Garden. Here is another way to put it:

"Has God really said you shall not eat of any tree in the Garden, or else you will die? [has God said "A"?] Surely you will not die ["non-A" is the truth]."

CHAPTER 6: RATIONAL CONVICTION

If we truly believe that wisdom and faith are exemplified by embracing irrationality, then Satan was faithful and wise in his admonition here. As well, if this is correct, Christians cannot believe a word that comes out of God's mouth. Rationality would say that whatever God says corresponds to reality ("A"="A"). But blind faith says truth can be irrational. Therefore, what God says (i.e., "truth") may not correspond to reality ("A" does not have to equal "A"). If this is the case, while God says that he loves you, wisdom says that love can equal non-love. While Christ says that he will never leave you or forsake you, true faith says that not forsaking can equal forsaking. Sorry for belaboring this, but here is my point: if rationality is not a rule that God has to go by because he is God, then our faith is in vain. There is no hope.

Our faith is rational precisely because God is rational. We are to believe rationally because God has created us, in his image, as rational beings. While it is correct that truth is often beyond our ability to rationally comprehend it (truth is trans-rational), this does not make it irrational in any sense.

Irrational Conviction

The Belief-O-Meter below illustrates the faith of one whose beliefs are completely irrational. Look it over for a bit.

I am going to use a biblical illustration for this one. In Isaiah 40-48, God condemns the Israelites for their faith in other gods. It might be better to say he belittles them for their irrationality. They had turned from their trust in God and begun to trust other gods for their needs.

Again, this meter represents the irrational faith of the Israelites. Notice the sub-meters. The "real life" experience meter is active, due to their experience with other gods. They may have prayed to the goddess of fertility and nine months later had a child. They may have prayed to the rain god and within an hour it rained. The "referred" meter is high because so many of those who the Israelites knew worshiped other gods as well. It was a community thing. However, notice the main meter, which represents the amount of true biblical conviction they had. It is at zero. Why? Because the rational meter is at zero, meaning that their faith was completely irrational. No matter what your personal experience, no matter what your friends and family believe, no matter what the philosophers of the day are saying, if it is irrational, it is not of God.

I love how God talks to the Israelites. Not only does it tell me that God has a great sense of humor, but it also shows that God calls on us to use our minds and not take leaps of faith.

Isa. 40:18-21
To whom then will you liken God, or what likeness compare with him? 19 An idol! A craftsman casts it, and a goldsmith overlays it with gold and casts for it silver chains. 20 He who is too impoverished for an offering chooses wood that will not rot; he seeks out a skillful craftsman to set up an idol that will not move. 21 Do you not know? Do you not hear? Has it not been told you from the beginning? Have you not understood from the foundations of the earth?

God is challenging the Israelites to *think* about what they are doing. He wants them to compare their gods to him. He introduces the characters involved in idolatry. It is significant that the idol's various creators are spoken of. We have a craftsman who creates the idol and a goldsmith who decorates it. It is important to realize that the idol is completely dependent on the craftsman and the goldsmith to create it. It is through *their* power and *their* creativity that the idol exists! And it is in their own creation that they put their trust? Notice the repetition: "Do you not *know*. Do you not *hear*? .

CHAPTER 6: RATIONAL CONVICTION

. . Have you not *understood* from the foundations of the earth?" Know, hear, and understand. This is what God is asking Israel to do. Think! Use your minds!

"From the foundations of the earth" draws attention to the fact that rational thinking is not something that has to be revealed in time from God. It has been innate to man since the beginning. It is *common* sense.

He goes on:

Isaiah 41:7
The craftsman encourages the goldsmith, and he who smooths with the hammer spurs on him who strikes the anvil. He says of the welding, "It is good." He nails down the idol so it will not topple.

Notice the mockery here. The man who is creating this *god* has to nail it down on the platform so that when they are carrying it, it does not fall! It is dependent on man for its ability to stand against the perils of gravity, yet man is going to depend on it for everything else?

God continues:

Isa 41:22-23
"Bring in your idols to tell us what is going to happen. Tell us what the former things were, so that we may consider them and know their final outcome. Or declare to us the things to come, 23 tell us what the future holds, so we may know that you are gods. Do something, whether good or bad, so that we will be dismayed and filled with fear.

Here God compares his knowledge with the impotent minds of the idols. God has declared the future, which gives rationale for belief in his deity. Only a God who transcends time can tell the future. God does tell the future; therefore, God is the only God. God asks the Israelites, "What is your *rationale* for worshiping these other gods?"

And there is more:

Isa 44:12-19
The blacksmith takes a tool and works with it in the coals; he shapes an idol with hammers, he forges it with the might of his arm. He gets hungry and loses his strength; he drinks no water and grows faint. 13 The carpenter measures with a line and makes an outline with a marker; he roughs it out with chisels and marks it with compasses. He shapes it in the form of man, of man in all his glory, that it may dwell in a shrine. 14 He cut down cedars, or perhaps it was a cypress or oak. He let it grow among the trees of the forest, or planted a pine, and the rain made it grow. 15 It is man's fuel for burning; some of it he takes and warms himself, he kindles a fire and bakes bread. But he also fashions a god and worships it; he makes an idol and bows down to it. 16 Half of the wood he burns in the fire; over it he prepares his meal, he roasts his meat and eats his fill. He also warms himself and says, "Ah! I am warm; I see the fire." 17 From the rest he makes a god, his idol; he bows down to it and worships. He prays to it and says, "Save me; you are my god. 18 "They know nothing, they understand nothing; their eyes are plastered over so they cannot see, and their minds closed so they cannot understand. 19 No one stops to think, no one has the knowledge or understanding to say, "Half of it I used for fuel; I even baked bread over its coals, I roasted meat and I ate. Shall I make a detestable thing from what is left? Shall I bow down to a block of wood?"

You see how God belittles of this kind of faith? It is completely irrational. God made the trees grow. The craftsman chose a tree and cut it down. The "strong" man creating the idol got tired while creating it. I love it! Can you imagine someone creating a god and having to stop due to fatigue? "Hey, get me that towel so I can wipe off my forehead. It is hot in here. Also, can you bring me a jug of water? This god-making is exhausting." Once he is done, he takes the idol's brother and sister (the other blocks of wood) and starts a fire with it. He uses one piece of wood as his own servant to keep him warm, but the other he bows down to, asking it to save him! Irrationality at its best.

CHAPTER 6: RATIONAL CONVICTION

Notice: irrational thinking, in God's estimation, is not wisdom and is certainly not pleasing to him. God hates blind faith. He says, "No one stops to *think*." No one pulls over and says, "Hey, wait a minute. Does this really make sense?"

There is no virtue in blind faith. There is no virtue in irrationality. A truly biblical faith will not be irrational. God calls on us to use our minds to think. The creature cannot make the creator. That is a contradiction. God does not work through contradictions and does not contradict himself.

We, as Christians, are called upon to love God with all our hearts, souls, and minds (Matt. 22:37). We are to love him with the way we believe. An irrational faith is a blind faith. Of course, not all of our faith will be intuitive, but it certainly will not be irrational or logically absurd. Let us get used to a faith that engages the mind. While we will never be able to look God eye-to-eye in our reasoning, God is certainly not scared of our questions.

Discussion Questions:

1. What is the most irrational thing you have done in your life? What made it irrational?

2. If we were to concede that God can contradict himself, what promises would be in jeopardy?

3. How is believing in an eternal transcendent God rational?

4. How is atheism (disbelief in God) irrational?

5. What ways does the church today promote irrationality?

6. In what ways can we increase our rational conviction of our faith?

Keeping the Big Picture:

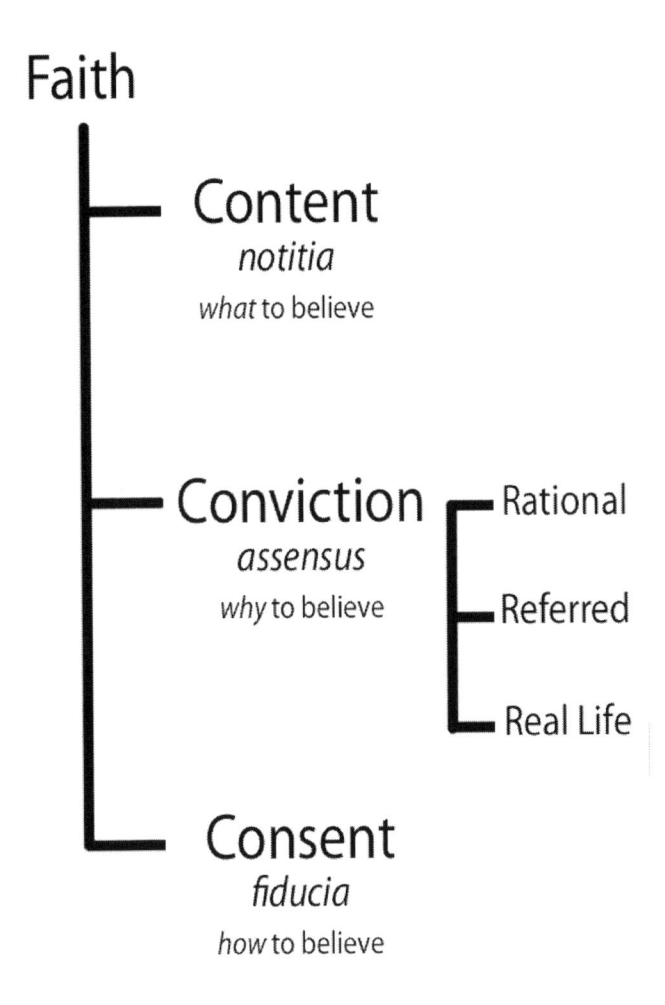

Faith
- **Content**
  notitia
  what to believe
- **Conviction** — Rational
  assensus   — Referred
  why to believe — Real Life
- **Consent**
  fiducia
  how to believe

CHAPTER #7

ADDING EVIDENCE TO OUR CONVICTION

(Warning: Santa Clause spoiler forthcoming)

I have to admit it. While growing up, Santa Clause was my favorite Saint (although at four years old, I did not know he was a Saint, nor did I care). He was the guy who partnered up with mom and dad and brought me presents for Christmas. I believed in him because mom and dad said he was real. In fact, I saw him once. It had to be after midnight. I sat in my bed, anxiously trying to force sleep to pass the time until we could burst into the dimly lit living room with shouts of joy and excitement when we heard some bells. I low-crawled down the hall with my little sister. We took a shortcut through the dining room and peered toward the Christmas tree. There he was! He had lost some weight and had something seriously wrong with his beard, but it was him nonetheless. Santa Clause was at our house! He told us to get to bed. His voice was strangely similar to my father's, and he was not very jolly. No matter. I wanted to believe, therefore I was willing to suspend any sort of critical spirit that fought to have a voice.

As the years passed, my desire to believe in him continued, but some

CHAPTER 7: ADDING EVIDENCE TO OUR CONVICTION

things were not adding up. Sure, the cookies and milk I set out for him each year were gone every Christmas morning. As well, I could not deny the fact that there were gifts under the tree on Christmas morning that were not there the night before. And these presents were different, mind you. A key sign at our house that a particular present was from Santa was that the gift was unwrapped. Not to mention, my most trusted sources for referred conviction (mom and dad) still insisted he was real. I had plenty of reasons to continue to believe, but there were some things that, again, were not adding up.

Kristie and Angie, my older sisters, provided a very disturbing testimony. They told me more than once, in confidence, that Santa was not real. While I thought they were crazy, they did throw a wrench in the stability of my referred conviction. According to their account of things, mom and dad were Santa Claus. I wondered if others shared their crazy worldview. This took me back to my encounter with Santa that night. My sisters' testimony made sense following my observation that Santa sounded like my dad. Of course, the more I thought about it, it *was* possible that mom and dad ate the cookies and drank the milk. After all, they had to eat and drink too. And my dad *really* liked cookies. It was well within their capabilities to place unwrapped Christmas presents under the tree. Not only this, but it made little sense that Santa could make it to every house in the world in one night, especially if he was going as slowly as he was the night I saw him.

The kicker came the following year. I was on the pre-Christmas hunt for mom's gift hiding place. Rumor had it that it was in the south hallway closet. Though it was normally always locked, on this particular day it was not. When I looked inside, to this seven-year-old boy's horror, there lay Santa's suit, boots, and white beard. It was almost final. I just had to get mom and dad to admit their deception and I could put a nail in this coffin, count my losses, and confirm my broken heart. Although my mother attempted to stand her ground for a time, the overwhelming amount of evidence eventually caused her concession. Since that day, I have not believed in Santa.

We will get back to ol' Saint Nick in a moment!

Real Life Conviction (*evidentia*)

Real life conviction. That *might* not be the best way to put it, but it does begin with an "R"! Reviewing from an earlier chapter, this most broadly refers to human *experience*. It is often called "empirical," meaning that which we can observe or experience through our senses. It has to do with the *evidence*. Appropriately, the Reformers called this, along with rational conviction, *evidentia*. It is stuff that we can see, feel, taste, touch, or test. This can come by way of direct personal encounters, or by historical or empirical verification. Whereas rational conviction comes intuitively and works primarily off of logical deduction, real life conviction comes by way of subjective encounter, evidence, and testing. It is induction. It makes up the third sub-meter in our "conviction meter." It is a very important part of our faith.

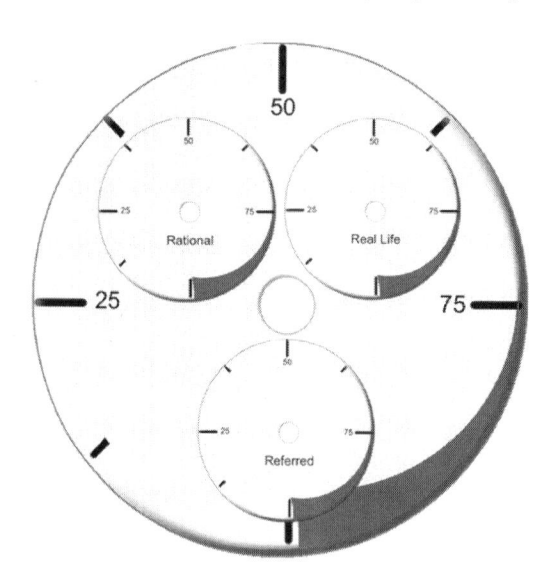

During the Enlightenment, there were two schools of thought about where our ultimate source of information came from: the "Rationalists" and the "Empiricists." The rationalists believed our most important type of knowledge was intuitive, meaning that we are born preprogrammed with paradigms of understanding. The empiricists believed our ultimate source of knowledge was from real world evidence. These would be the things we learn through real life experience and investigation. In essence, this is the age-old nature vs. nurture debate; the philosopher vs. the scientist. Do we know what we know due to our inherent nature (rationalism), or do we know what we know due to life's nurturing (empiricism)?

CHAPTER 7: ADDING EVIDENCE TO OUR CONVICTION

The folly in the rationalism vs. empiricism debate comes when we exclude one or the other. The truth is that *both* are important components in our knowledge, conviction, and faith. We are born with a certain rational framework that guides and applies the information we acquire later in life. Even the scientist who says, "This is my method: I believe in only what I can see and what I can test" (often referred to as "Logical Positivism"), cannot be consistent. Why? Because *this very method* cannot be seen or tested! Does the scientist believe in this method? Maybe, but it is a *rational* conviction which cannot be put under the microscope. It is intuitive, not empirical. This is what philosophers call a self-defeating belief. It's like saying "My wife has never been married." A wife, by definition, must be married. In the same way, the method of those who say, "I *only* believe in that which I can empirically verify" is self-defeating since one cannot empirically verify the truth of such a statement.

However, our experience provides a powerful guide that can help us to adjust our way of thinking at a fundamental level. It is much easier to believe things that we can test and experience. This is the stuff of "real life."

How Real Life Conviction Works

When I believed in Santa, I had to look for evidence to help confirm my belief; it was ultimately the lack of evidence that ended that belief. Initially, I had testimony from others (referred conviction, based purely on mom's and dad's authority). This is how my faith in Santa looked at first:

Notice the rational meter is slightly raised. Intuitively, by itself, there is nothing *formally* absurd with a belief in a guy with superpowers, giving presents to all children. It is logically *possible*.

However, there is nothing that would intuitively compel anyone in such a direction either. In other words, it is not logically necessary. Therefore, the rational meter has very little to say here. The referred meter, on the other hand, is very high. Most of my faith in Santa had come from mom and dad's testimony. Most of the other kids my age believed in him too. Therefore, there was a confirmation of prejudice on the playground! But notice the real life meter. It is not too high. The evidences, while present, were not above reproach at all.

Now I am going to introduce into the Real Life meter two sub-meters. Please hang with me.

1. First-hand Evidence (or Personal Experience)

First-hand evidence is composed of those things we personally experience. Left unchecked, this, along with emotions (which I will talk about in the section on consent) is the most powerful of all the contributors to our belief. Many people work *only* off this. These are the things that *we* touch, taste, smell, hear, and see. Speaking of Santa, my first-hand experience came when I actually heard the bells and saw Santa by the tree. With regard to our faith in God, these are the experiences we have that confirm our worldview. These would include miracles, answers to prayer, visions, and other encounters with what we believe are best explained through a divine agency.

2. Forensic Evidence

These are the breadcrumbs of our faith. Anyone who is hooked on one of the crime investigation television series knows what I am talking about. Forensic science deals with evidence, which confirms or denies the presupposition. In other words, while first-hand evidence sees a man walk through the snow, forensic evidence looks at the footprints left behind. With regard to Santa, my forensic evidence was the presents under the tree Christmas morning, which were not present the night before. Forensic evidence has a historical element to it. It deals with shadows of the past – what we would expect to *have happened* if our belief is true. What evidence was left

CHAPTER 7: ADDING EVIDENCE TO OUR CONVICTION

behind? Are there alternative explanations for this evidence? With regard to our Christian faith, there are many evidences we would expect to find such as human design, innate morality, archaeological confirmation, historical impact and longevity, an empty tomb, devoted followers, and first-hand testimony.

Since much of the Christian faith is based on the testimony of others, some will equate this type of conviction with "Referred Conviction" (which we will talk about in the next chapter), but I think they are different. Referred Conviction is reliance on others' *conviction*, which becomes our own based on their scholarship and integrity. What I am talking about here is *evidence*, based on actions and beliefs that we would expect others to have if our faith is true.

Therefore, our Real Life conviction meter looks like this:

God and Real Life Evidence

When it comes to Christian belief, we must recognize that one's conviction level cannot be determined by Rational or Real Life conviction *alone* (as with the rationalists vs. empiricists mentioned earlier). We must have both. We have dogs in both hunts. The Bible shows that God calls on us to "come and see." As well, our Christian faith will be strengthened the more we focus on Real Life conviction, looking to both forensic and first-hand experiences.

According to the Christian worldview, God does not hide in the heavens, having already installed in every human all that is needed for conviction about his reality and his will. He intervenes in time, giving evidences of his presence, love, and redemption. We are not left to blindly grope in the dark, hoping to pin the tail on the right donkey.

The Bible tells us God has placed his fingerprints on his work (just like the footprints in the snow we discussed earlier). In his Gospel, John tell his readers that Jesus did many things during his life, but the selected biography was given so that people would be compelled *by the evidence given* to believe that Christ is the Son of God.

John 20:30-31
Now Jesus performed many other miraculous signs in the presence of the disciples, which are not recorded in this book. 31 But these are recorded so that you may believe that Jesus is the Christ, the Son of God, and that by believing you may have life in his name.

Luke, a contemporary of the Apostles and writer of the Gospel of Luke, tells his friend Theophilus that he *investigated* the events of Christ's life, death, and resurrection closely. It is upon this investigation that Luke's conviction and testimony are based.

Luke 1:1-4
Inasmuch as many have undertaken to compile an account of the things accomplished among us, 2 just as they were handed down to us by those who from the beginning were eyewitnesses and servants of the word, 3 it seemed fitting for me as well, having investigated everything carefully from the beginning, to write it out for you in consecutive order, most excellent Theophilus; 4 so that you may know the exact truth about the things you have been taught.

And we dare not forget the biggest skeptic in the Bible. Thomas, an apostle of Christ, having received the testimony from others (and possibly even seeing the empty tomb), would not believe that Christ had risen from the grave until he (empirically) saw him and touched his wounds.

CHAPTER 7: ADDING EVIDENCE TO OUR CONVICTION

John 20:25
So the other disciples were saying to him, "We have seen the Lord!" But he said to them, "Unless I see in His hands the imprint of the nails, and put my finger into the place of the nails, and put my hand into His side, I will not believe.

Sure enough, eight days later, Thomas got his wish and was finally convinced by the first-hand evidence that Christ rose from the grave (John 20:26-28).

As well, when Christ rose from the grave, he did not do so in secret, informing someone many years later through an angelic encounter. He could have just gone up into heaven and required blind faith of all his followers. But, according to Luke, Christ was actively teaching immediately after his resurrection, presenting himself to his followers by "many convincing proofs" (Acts 1:3).

In Acts 17, Paul tells the philosophers at Mars Hill that God has given evidence for himself so that we would not be groping in the dark.

Acts 17:24-28
The God who made the world and all things in it, since He is Lord of heaven and earth, does not dwell in temples made with hands; 25 nor is He served by human hands, as though He needed anything, since He Himself gives to all people life and breath and all things; and he made from one man every nation of mankind to live on all the face of the earth, having determined allotted periods and the boundaries of their dwelling place, 27 that they should seek God, in the hope that they might feel their way toward him and find him. Yet he is actually not far from each one of us, 28 for "In him we live and move and have our being"; as even some of your own poets have said, "For we are indeed his offspring."

God is close to us, having provided evidence for his existence and activity. Though he does not need man nor dwell with man, he is not far from any of us. He is present and active.

Many Christians fail to explore real-life conviction when exercising their faith. This can dramatically influence their conviction level. If we don't look toward the evidence God has provided through his fingerprints on history and in our own experience, our faith will be weakened.

Belief in Santa Claus is unwarranted, not because we don't want him to exist (for what child does not emotionally want to believe in Santa?), or even because it is rationally absurd, but because the evidence is simply not present. However, belief in God does not have to be like belief in Santa. We can – indeed, we are called upon – to investigate the claims of the Christian faith.

Also, as this whole process seems to get more complicated, I feel compelled to remind you that nothing I have said is necessarily rocket science. Think of this as an "anatomy of faith." For the most part, we are simply looking into how all of us already believe, even if we don't know these things. My purpose is to give you tools to either diagnose a problem you may have in our Christian belief, or to propel you forward in the same.

In the following chapters, we will look further into how both first-hand and forensic elements to Real Life conviction add to the testimony of Christianity.

Discussion Questions:

1. Does Real Life Conviction contribute to your faith? If so, in what ways?

2. Further explain how belief in God and belief in Santa are different.

CHAPTER 7: ADDING EVIDENCE TO OUR CONVICTION

3. Describe how your faith might suffer if your conviction is only based on rational conviction.

4. Describe how your faith might suffer if your conviction is only based on referred conviction.

5. Why do you think that Luke examined the evidence so closely when writing his Gospel? Isn't this a lack of faith?

Keeping the Big Picture:

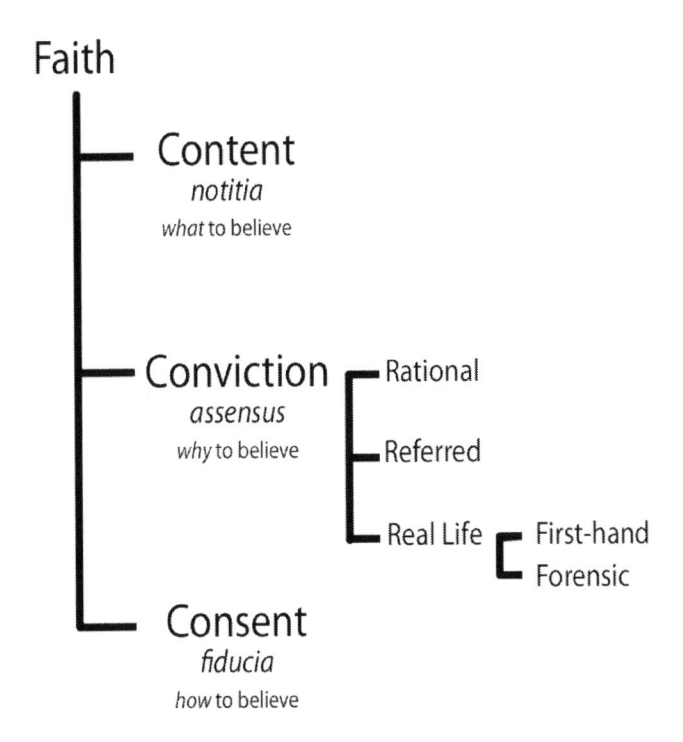

Faith

- **Content**
  notitia
  what to believe

- **Conviction**
  assensus
  why to believe
  - Rational
  - Referred
  - Real Life
    - First-hand
    - Forensic

- **Consent**
  fiducia
  how to believe

CHAPTER #8

FIRST-HAND FAITH

I have a few confessions to make: I have never heard God's voice. I don't know what he smells like. I have not seen him with my eyes and my hands have never held his. I have never seen anyone brought back from the dead. I have never seen anyone healed of any disease. I have never seen a blind man see or a deaf man hear. Let's just get that out on the table. If my convictions about God were limited to things such as these, I doubt I would have much faith.

I remember when I was twelve years old, God peeked out of the shroud of experiential darkness. This is going to sound silly to a lot of you, but it was special to me nonetheless. I was at the Quail Creek Elementary School carnival. All of us went back to it for years after "graduating" elementary school (to show how cool us "post-grads" were). Each year at the carnival they had a cakewalk. You know, the game where you walk around a circle of 36 numbers while music plays. When the music stops, you stop. If you are on the number they call, you win a cake. At that point in my life, I had never won anything (that I can remember), but I really wanted to win this cake, so I did what any twelve-year-old Christian would do: I prayed. "Dear God, if you are listening, please show me by allowing me to

CHAPTER 8: FIRST-HAND FAITH

win this cake. Amen." The music played. I walked. The music stopped. I stopped. They called out "32." I looked down. I was on 32. Wow! It was something special. God made me win the cakewalk. He *really* did care! He was *really* there. The next year, same time, same place, same prayer. And you know what? I won again. It was unbelievable to this now 13-year-old kid. It was a miracle! God was indeed on my side.

The next year, I went again. I felt like I was going to meet God at *our* special place. It was like a date with the Almighty. I was so excited. It was a great confirmation to my faith for him to take the time to peer out from behind the clouds. Two years before, you could have asked me, "Why do you believe in God, Michael?" I might have said, "Because my mom says he is real." But now you could ask the same question and I would say, "Because he gets me a cake each year. How else do you explain my victories?" There I was, nervous and giddy. The music started playing and I started praying. The music stopped. I stopped. "Number 12," the lady called out. *There must be some mistake,* I thought to myself. *I am on 20.* I decided to try again, this time tagging the ol' faithful "in Jesus' name" to the end of my prayer. "Number 5," she announced. I was on 8. Something had gone seriously wrong. Maybe God was not going to show up. Maybe the other two times were just coincidences. I went home with my head hanging low, not sure how to believe.

"God Things"

Have you ever heard the phrase "It's a God thing?" "God things" are those experiences we cannot explain outside of God's direct intervention. When we meet someone by "chance" and this encounter turns out to be something that changes our lives, it's a "God thing." When we forget our cell phone at home and have to go back only to find out that we left the stove on, it's a "God thing." One of my favorite movies of all time is *Signs* with Mel Gibson. It is all about "God things." There is one scene where Mel Gibson, a priest who has lost his faith, asks his brother if he believes that God works miracles or if the things we cannot explain are just coincidences. His brother tells a story about sitting next to a girl at a party and leaning in to kiss her. He then realizes he has gum in his mouth. He turns to take it out, and by the time he turns back around, she is throwing up all over the place. He said, "I could have been kissing her when she threw up. I'm a miracle man." To him, that was a "God thing."

Personal experience is an important part of our conviction. We want to have "God things" in our lives to confirm our beliefs. To have God speak to us from heaven, to have been around when Christ walked the earth, to have seen the Red Sea part, there would have been no denying "God things." And if there are "God things," then there is a God. It's a simple two-step deduction.

To be truthful, I don't know of many things in my life that I can *conclusively* say were "God things." Don't get me wrong. I believe I have experienced many "God things." But when push comes to shove, someone could argue that these events were just coincidences. Because of this, I don't rest too heavily on my particular interpretation of life's events or base my faith in God *exclusively* on such things.

My real life conviction meter often looks like this:

Notice that while I have a lot of "forensic" conviction for Christianity (next chapter), my first-hand experience meter is quite lacking. This is why my overall real-life meter is not as high as I would like.

Making the Two-Dimensional Three-Dimensional

We are talking about the

anatomy of belief, if you will. First-hand experiences, while they should not be *the* hinges of our faith, do act as screws in the hinges. And they are nice to have. I often said experiences make that which would otherwise be two-dimensional, three-dimensional.

In the human body, while basic anatomical structures are shared by all of us, those structures can vary with regard to their strengths and weaknesses. I have a good friend who is about my age who has been plagued with heart problems for years. Sometimes it keeps him in bed for days. My heart, as far as I know, is perfectly healthy. I don't know why he suffers from this problem while I don't. I, on the other hand, have weak joints and a terribly bad back. Those of you who have bad backs know how debilitating this can be. Others never have joint or back problems.

It is not so different when it comes to our faith. People's faith will be strong in some areas and weak in others. Some people seem to experience God in ways that make me drool. They are the ones who have all the answered prayers, see the miracles, and win all the cakewalks! I often lean on their experiences and drink their water in the areas of my faith that often seem to be in perpetual drought.

A Man Who Died and Found His Conviction

The power of personal experience is undeniable. Lives can be dramatically changed by just one experience. They can often jump-start our faith and move us in the right direction.

I talked to a man the other day who told me the story of his life. He had been a believer growing up, but had left the faith as he got into the world of academics. While he was a college professor, he remained a Christian in name only. He eventually rejected just about everything he had been taught as a child, believing it to be nonsense. Late in his life, when he was about sixty, he had a heart attack and died. According to his testimony, he left his body and went to heaven. While there, he experienced the reality of the presence of God. He was brought back to life a changed man.

Now, please understand, I am a hopeless skeptic about these types of things. I would like to believe in them. The problem is, when I hear these stories, they often don't add up. Many times, the heaven they describe is an unbiblical portrait of the afterlife. Other times, the people who die and go to heaven are not even Christians! So while I don't doubt the *sincerity* of such stories, I don't really know how to assimilate them into my belief either. However (and this is the main point), this man's experience became the bedrock of his faith. Since being brought back to life, he has followed the Lord with great passion. His conviction was supported by what he believed happened (and maybe it did happen, I don't know). The academic problems he had (represented by the forensic meter) were no match for his near-death *experience*. In fact, those academic problems, for better or worse, were simply rethought being now filtered by his experience of heaven. After this, what had previously seemed intellectually unlikely became probable.

Here is what I *imagine* his conviction meter looked like immediately after his experience.

Notice his forensic meter is still low. Remember, he lost his faith in academics. However, his first-hand meter is high due to his near-death experience. The overall real-life conviction meter is up, but not too high.

After some time processing this event, this gentleman probably reassessed his previous beliefs, being encouraged and confirmed by his near-death experience. After about six months of reflection and further studies, I *imagine* this is how his conviction meter looked.

CHAPTER 8: FIRST-HAND FAITH

Now his forensic meter is on the rise and with it, the overall real life meter. His experience jump-started his faith in one area, but it affected everything. Again, if you remember, the "Real Life" conviction meter is only one of the three meters that make up our overall conviction. The other two, "Rational" and "Referred", are not in the picture here. However, the way the anatomy of faith works, one sub-meter will eventually affect all the others. I imagine that, based on this experience, he reassessed his rational and referred convictions as well.

This represents the power (though not necessarily the validity) these types of experiences can have on our life. In Christianity, we often call them "Damascus Road experiences," for that is where Paul met with Christ – an experience that undoubtedly changed the course of Paul's entire life (Acts 9:1-8).

The Bible and First-Hand Conviction

While they are wonderful and powerful, we still need to be very careful about relying on first-hand experiences to fuel our conviction. They are the most volatile of all. They are readily misinterpreted and easy to forget. They can also become like a drug to which we become addicted. In short, first-hand experiences need to be supported by the other areas of our faith, not be the *sole* catalyst for our trust.

For Christians, God's silence – often called God's "hiddenness" – should not come as any surprise. Granted, if I had a say, I might do things differently. Were I on God's board of directors, I might give him some gentle encouragement to be a little more open to showing himself, especially to his own children. I might say, "Come on God. Just let him win one more cakewalk. How hard is that?" But the fact is we should not expect to win every cakewalk. While we will experience God in many ways, I do not believe we will see him, hear him, or touch him in the way we often desire. In fact, if we did, I believe the Christian worldview would be compromised. Why? Because Scripture tells us we should not expect to have our faith confirmed through such empirical means.

1 Pet. 1:8-9
And though you have not seen Him, you love Him, and though you do not see Him now, but believe in Him, you greatly rejoice with joy inexpressible and full of glory, obtaining as the outcome of your faith the salvation of your souls.

You see, here Peter assumes that we have not seen Christ (or God or the Holy Spirit for that matter). That is, we have not seen him visually. Peter's point would be moot if he did not mean to include all other forms of experiencing God *empirically*. Think about it. Peter was not saying, "And though you have not seen him, you love him. (But many of you will hear, touch, and smell him)." The point is that we should not expect to have *that type* of confirmation of his reality. The fact is, when Christ ascended into heaven, that became the last time most of us on earth would see or *hear* him *in such a way*. Please note (and please bear with me as I belabor this point) I did not say, "That was the last time he was active in an evident way." There is a big difference. The point is that we should not expect to *directly* experience God through our eyes, ears, or hands until Christ returns. Whether we like it or not, there is a certain degree of silence which appears to be his M.O. for now.

Remember when Thomas demanded to see the risen Christ before he would believe?

John 20:27-29
Then He said to Thomas, "Reach here with your finger, and see My hands; and reach here your hand and put it into My side; and do not be unbelieving, but believing." 28 Thomas answered and said to Him, "My Lord and my God!" 29 Jesus said to him, "Because you have seen Me, have you believed? Blessed are they who did not see, and yet believed."

Blessed are those who did not see, yet believed. Christ knew that, following his ascension, the majority of the world would have to base their conviction on things other than first-hand experiences. In other words, belief – *strong* belief – is possible without them. There is much more to the anatomy of our faith than these types of experiences.

Seeing the Angels

I am reminded of the story in which the prophet Elisha was being hunted by the king of Aram. The king's army surrounded the city where Elisha and his servant were resting. Elisha's servant went into a panic, while Elisha remained calm. There was something happening that his servant was unable to experience. Something Elisha saw stabilized his faith. Elisha prayed for his servant's eyes to be opened.

2 Kings 6:17
Then Elisha prayed and said, "O LORD, I pray, open his eyes that he may see." And the LORD opened the servant's eyes and he saw; and behold, the mountain was full of horses and chariots of fire all around Elisha.

There were angels surrounding Elisha and his servant! Only his servant could not see the angels.

While I have given some warnings about seeking to build your faith *solely* on first-hand experience, I do not mean to imply we should be afraid to seek such experiences. I believe it is godly and important for us to pray that we recognize the "God things." They are all around us, even if they can often suffer alternative explanations. Often, we just need to have our eyes opened.

For the most part, is not going to be our sight that brings conviction to our faith, but our conviction that brings reality to our sight. I think that is the most important thing I have said here so I will repeat it: It is not going to be our sight that brings conviction to our faith, but our conviction that brings reality to our sight. As C.S. Lewis once said, "I believe in Christianity as I believe that the Sun has risen, not only because I see it, but because by it I see everything else" ("Is Theology Poetry?" in The Weight of Glory: And Other Addresses [New York: HarperCollins, 2001], 140).

Some people's first-hand experience of God will make us jealous. We will wonder why God is not so "conversational" with us. Many will see "angels" everywhere they turn. They will be at no loss for cakes. "God things" will be in abundance throughout their lives.

Many times it is just a matter of perspective. We need to open our eyes in faith. For many of us, God, for some mysterious reason, goes into hiding in this area. This can be frustrating, I know. "Just let me win one more darn cakewalk. How hard is that?" But first-hand experience should only be one aspect of our faith. We take what we can get, but our faith does not need to suffer because of a lack of this one thing.

If your first-hand experience meter is low and it does not look like it is going to change, join the crowd of many strong believers throughout history who have complained about God's hiddenness. The first-hand meter will never be at full-throttle until we stand before God. Once that happens, I suspect the other meters will not matter. Until then, seek to have your eyes opened, but don't lean too heavily on experience alone. There is so much more that can stabilize our faith. As well, be encouraged (not jealous) of others with whom God does seem to have an experiential open line. God may have placed them in your life to provide what is lacking in your faith.

Discussion Questions:

1. Name some times when you have had "God things" happen to you.

2. Why do you think that God stay silent for so many Christians?

3. Why is experience such a powerful driving force for our faith?

4. Explain how experience might lead you in the wrong direction?

5. Who are some people that you believe have had "God things" happen to them? How does this help your faith?

Keeping the Big Picture:

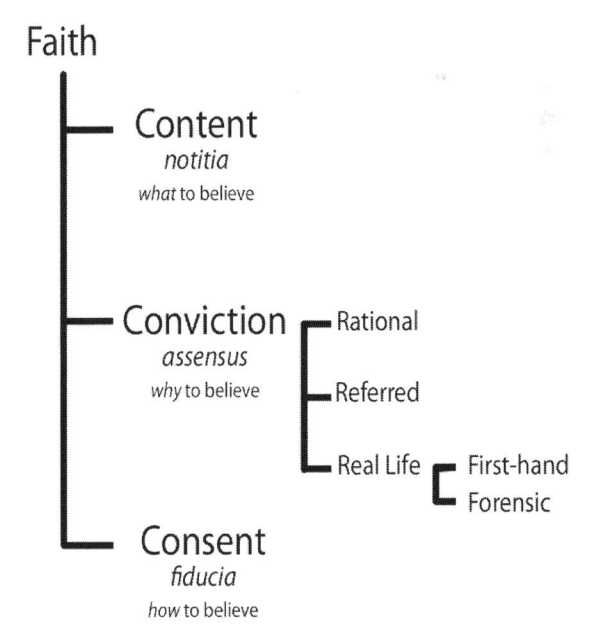

Faith
- Content
  notitia
  what to believe

- Conviction — Rational
  assensus — Referred
  why to believe — Real Life — First-hand
                                    — Forensic

- Consent
  fiducia
  how to believe

CHAPTER #9

FORENSIC EVIDENCE FOR CHRIST AND FOR THE DEATH OF MY SISTER

My sister Angie died in January 2004. I believe this to be the case. In fact, I am so convicted of the veracity of her death, I say without hesitation that I am certain that she died. No, no . . . not in a mathematically certain sense. No, not in an *infallible* sense. For cases such as these are not like mathematics, and I am not infallible. Therefore, by definition, I *could* be wrong. But I am not. Angie is indeed dead.

(Please forgive the rather morbid illustration that I use here. I only include it because of its relevance to the issue at hand).

Let me tell you a bit of the story:

I got a phone call from the medical examiner while on Hwy 635 in Dallas, TX. I did not recognize the phone number, but I answered it anyway.

"Is this Michael Patton?" the voice said.

CHAPTER 9: FORENSIC EVIDENCE FOR CHRIST AND... 93

"Yes, it is," I responded with curiosity to this heavily-accented country voice.

"Are you in your car?"

"Yes, I am," I said, with an increasing amount of curiosity and a growing degree of fear.

"Is your family with you?" he asked.

"Yes, they are," I said, this time with more fear than curiosity.

"Could you pull over, please?" he requested.

By this point, I *knew* what was next.

Let me pause for a moment and let you in on something: I have never in my life had some random unidentified person call me and ask these questions while driving down the road. Neither have I received such a phone call since. And I hope I never do again. Just think about it. My cell phone rings in my car and an unfamiliar, heavily-accented voice that sounds like Brooks, Dunn, or Haggard asks me to pull over. What was I to think of that? Pull over? Why? There was a fleeting thought that popped in my mind. In retrospect, it was more hopeful than fleeting. I remember this thought because right after the request to pull over, I looked into the rear-view mirror to see if there was a police car behind me. But why would a policeman *call on my cell phone* to ask me to pull over? Normally they just turn on their lights. However, I knew better. I *hoped* for different (even the police!), but I knew better.

Back to the conversation:

"Why?" I responded to his request to pull over. "It's my sister, isn't it?" My overwhelming fear did not give him time to answer. I preempted him with another question. "She is dead, isn't she?"

After a long pause, the medical examiner responded, "Yes, sir."

I knew she was dead. Although I did not have any "hard" evidence, I was sure of what had happened. Angie, my sister, had committed suicide. I did not go to see the body. Though he told me where they found her (at a hotel in Denton, TX), I did not need to go there to examine the scene. Without hesitation or doubt, I immediately made the hardest phone call I have ever had to make: I called my mother and told her what happened. After I talked to my mom, I stopped by my house in Frisco, TX, to get some clothes, then began the three-hour drive back to our hometown, Oklahoma City, to mourn with my family. All of this I did because I implicitly trusted the unknown random voice on the other end of my cell phone that Wednesday evening.

Two days later, I headed back to Texas with my wife to pick up Angie's car and her cremated remains. As we pulled up to the medical examiner's office, my wife was gracious enough to go inside and do what needed to be done. I was too scared. When she came back, I anxiously asked her what she saw. She told me that they had pictures of the scene of Angie's death. She said that though there were many, she could not look at any of them but one. It was a picture of Angie's hand on a gun. She saw no face, no body, and no blood. Only her hand still gripping the gun.

"Are you sure it was her hand?" Now, you must understand, this was a question of desperation. I *knew* it was. "Yes, it was hers," my wife said, with a look on her face as if she felt she was taking away my last bit of hope. But I thought I might need more closure. So I immediately called the medical examiner from the parking lot and asked, "Can I come in and see the pictures myself?" I am sure he was thinking very carefully about how to respond and that is why he paused for a bit before answering. "Yes, you can come see them. *But* I don't think you want to." My heart sank with those words, knowing what they implied. "Remember her as she was," he continued. "Don't do this to yourself." I remember almost getting out of the car, but then sinking back into my seat. I conceded to his counsel.

Kristie had brought out a plain white cardboard box. It is supposed to have Angie's ashes in them. Even today, they sit at my mom's house on a shelf, twelve feet high in her living room. I have never looked at them.

I believe Angie is dead. I never saw her body. I never saw the "crime scene." I never saw any pictures. I never saw the gun she used. I never saw any fingerprint evidence. I never even *saw* the medical examiner. And I have never looked into that white cardboard box. But based on one conversation with a guy I don't know, and the testimony of my wife who only saw her hand, my conviction that Angie is dead is very strong. Every once in a while, I have this fleeting irrational hope that shows up in a dream that Angie is alive. She normally appears in some random place and we find out that it was all a big mistake. But those are dreams. The reality is that Angie died on January 4, 2004. I believe this.

Forensic Conviction

We are talking about the different components of belief. We are asking about the *why?* and *how?* of faith. More specifically, we are talking about the process of belief in relation to Christianity. Building upon the intellectual conviction aspect of belief, we now turn to what I call forensic conviction.

But as a bit of review, allow me to put this in context once again: Forensic conviction makes up the second half of our "Real Life" conviction meter.

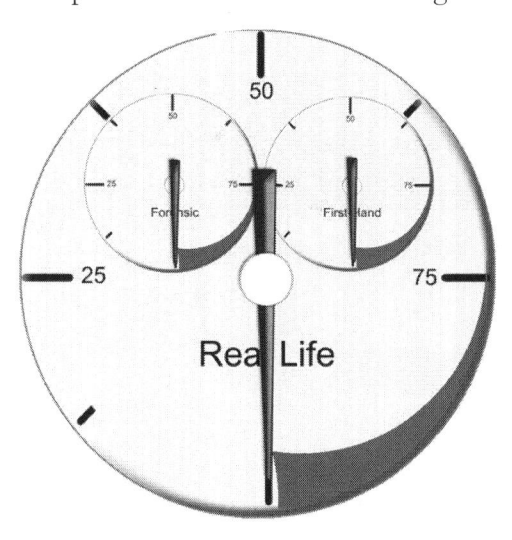

The real life conviction meter is one of three components that comprise our overall intellectual conviction. The conviction meter looks like this.

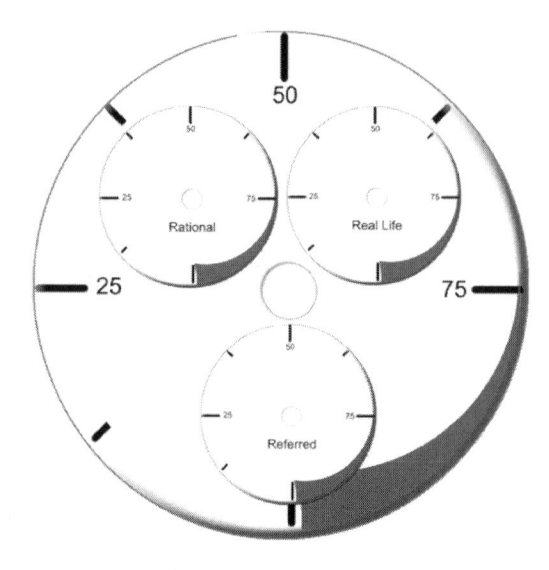

Finally, the conviction meter is one of three components that make up our overall belief.

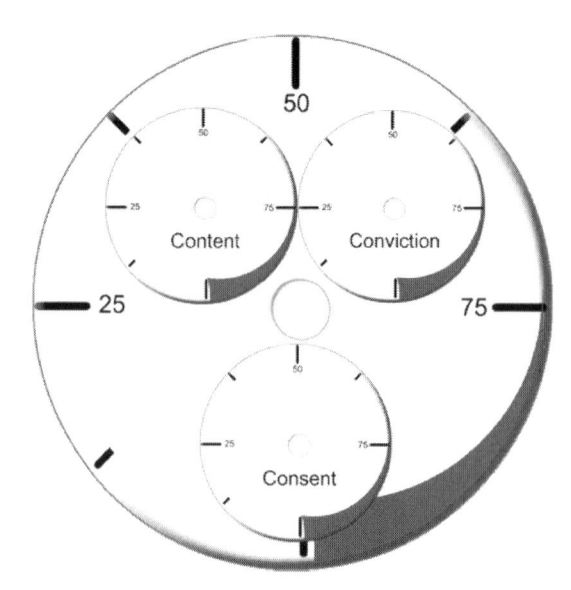

Forensic conviction is that aspect of our conviction which provides evidence for what we believe. In everyday usage, the word "forensic" relates to issues of forensic science (i.e. DNA, fingerprints, tire tracks, and the like). But we are not limiting it to such things here. The word "forensic" is taken from the Latin *forensis*, meaning "before the forum." It speaks to evidence one can bring to solidify a truth claim. Broadly, this can include any line of legitimate evidence that substantiates one's claims. It goes beyond first-hand evidence in that it looks to material, historical, and traditional forensic evidence.

As Christians, we believe many truth claims. It has been said before that many people believe things without any evidence at all, thinking any consideration of evidence is the polar opposite of faith. However, our conviction, while based on many things, must take into account the evidences for the veracity of our truth claims. Faith is very weak if it is blind. If God exists and has revealed himself in Jesus Christ, while we may not have been there to have first-hand conviction about such things, we can and should look to the fingerprints left behind.

This is often referred to as "Evidential Apologetics." "Apologetics" is taken from the Greek word *apologia*, used in 1 Peter 3:15, where Peter tells his readers to "always be ready to give a reason (apologia) for hope that is within you to everyone who asks." An apologist is one who spends his time constructing arguments *based on evidence* to defend and strengthen what he believes. While this book is not an apologetics book per se, it is an attempt to encourage the type of thinking and conviction that apologetics provides.

Evidence and the Resurrection of Christ

The central truth claim for Christianity is the resurrection of Christ. Paul tells the Corinthians that if Christ has not been raised from the grave, we should all just pack our bags and go home (or something like that).

1 Cor. 15:13-19
But if there is no resurrection of the dead, not even Christ has been raised; 14 and if Christ has not been raised, then our preaching is vain, your faith also is vain. 15 Moreover we are even found to be false witnesses of God, because we testified against God that He raised Christ, whom He did not raise, if in fact the dead are not raised. 16 For if the dead are not raised, not even Christ has been raised; 17 and if Christ has not been raised, your faith is worthless; you are still in your sins. 18 Then those also who have fallen asleep in Christ have perished.19 If we have hoped in Christ in this life only, we are of all men most to be pitied.

While our faith is "worthless" without Christ's resurrection, conversely, we believe that if Christ *did* rise from the grave, our faith is the opposite of worthless. It is the paradigm of all history. It demands all our allegiance and devotion. If Christ has risen from the grave, the implications are beyond tremendous.

However, none of us were there when Christ rose and, I assume, none of us have personally seen the risen Christ (1 Pet. 1:8). You cannot search YouTube for official *or* rogue footage of Christ's resurrection. Therefore, we have to look beyond first-hand evidence to substantiate our convictions. This is the way it is when we believe all matters of ancient history. It is important for us, then, to look for the fingerprints of the resurrection so that we can add forensic conviction to our belief.

The Resurrection of Christ and the Death of My Sister

As I said before, I believe my sister died in 2004. I have a strong conviction about this and I believe this conviction is warranted. In fact, I believe that it is so warranted that if I did not accept it as the truth, I would need to be assigned to a therapist for treatment. Granted, my conviction could be stronger. If I had gone into the medical examiner's office and seen the pictures myself I would have even more conviction. If I had been there when she died, I would be *even more* convicted. But I do not need these things to be secure in my belief that Angie died.

You see, Angie was living with me for many months prior to her suicide. Her life had taken many unfortunate turns. She had become severely depressed. About a year before her death, she had attempted suicide. I know this because I found her motionless in her bed. I carried her limp body out to my car, took her to the hospital, and watched as they treated her. Since that time she was on "suicide watch" in our family. In fact, the night I got the call from the medical examiner, my family and I believed that something was not right. No one could get ahold of her. I was actually out looking for her at the time I got the call, already fearing the worst. Therefore, I trusted that medical examiner without much question. I believed my wife when she said it was Angie's hand in the picture. I trust that the ashes at my mother's house are Angie's ashes. The fact that I have not seen Angie since that day further confirms my conviction. This is what we call circumstantial and corroborating evidence. *There are certain things that we would expect to find if said truth claim were really true.*

While you and I will not be able to have first-hand evidence, or even photographs, of Christ's resurrection, this does not mean that our conviction about Christ's resurrection has to suffer much. We simply look to the "footprints" of history. When it comes to Christ's resurrection, there are certain evidences which we should expect to find.

Let me list a few:

Contemporary documented evidence:

My conversation with the medical examiner that night, and with my wife in the medical examiner's parking lot, combined to give me much-needed contemporary evidence. Along with this comes my own testimony and understanding of Angie's volatile condition. I, a contemporary of the event (though not an eyewitness), have written about it many times on my blog. It had an incredible impact on my life. And here I am, many years later, still giving testimony to its reality.

If Christ rose from the grave, we would expect to find the same sort of accounting of the event and its immediate impact. Think about if an event such as this is claimed to have occurred and there was absolutely no record of it until hundreds of years later. For something as epic as someone claiming to be God's son dying and rising from the grave, it would be very hard to believe if contemporary testimony was not present. I would probably not believe it.

In the Bible, there are four accounts of Christ's life and death written within a generation of the event. These are called the "Gospels," meaning "good news." Each of these Gospels tells the same story, but are different enough for us to assume that there was no plot or collaboration to fabricate the event. As well, there is much evidence to believe that two of the Gospels (Matthew and John) were written by eyewitnesses. The other two, Mark and Luke, were written by contemporaries of the event. Luke even claims to have investigated everything closely (Luke 1:1-3). This would make him a key historical witness. This is what we would expect if Christ rose from the grave.

Near-contemporary collaboration and impact:

Since Angie's death, I have had many conversations with people who knew her, both friends and family. They all account for her absence with a belief in her death. In other words, no one has seen her or talked to her since that day. These individuals' knowledge of her past depression and present absence provides collaborating evidence. This is exactly what you would expect if Angie died.

Just as when you drop a boulder into a pond you get a ripple of waves, so also we would expect there to be ripples – indeed tidal waves – of residual impact from an event so monumental as the resurrection of someone who was the Son of God. Not only do we have contemporary testimony through the four Gospels, but we also have many more first-century documents which give account of or assume the resurrection of Christ. In the collection of documents we call the New Testament, we have twenty-two personal and public letters that give testimony to the impact of the resurrection on the near-contemporary society. Even outside of the New Testament, there are dozens of first and early-second century documents which assume the reality of the resurrection of Christ. These are from early believers, historians, pastors, philosophers, and even antagonists. Again, this is exactly what you would expect if Christ really rose from the grave.

Chronological and geographical information:

When I gave an account for Angie's death, I included places and times with a fair amount of detail. I said it happened on January 4, 2004. I talked about being on 635 in Dallas when I got the call from the medical examiner. I said they found her in a hotel in Denton. I talked about making the three-hour drive back to my hometown, Oklahoma City. In doing so, I opened the door for you to test one aspect of the veracity of my claim. If I were making this story up, I might have left those details out or replaced them with obscure places and times. That way you could not test my truth claim about Angie.

When a monumental event is claimed, it is very hard to believe if it was done in secret. Providing information about cities for which there is no record, kings who never ruled, and geographical sites that have no grounding in history is a sure way to ensure your story is labeled as myth. That is what you would do if you were making something up. That is what you would do if you were writing myth. However, if the testimony is true, one would expect the inclusion of details. Why? Because the one who is giving the account would not be afraid that his or her testimony would be debunked. When someone is fabricating a story, they can't provide these types of details, since there is a good chance others will check up on their accuracy. Surrounding the claims of the resurrection are an abundance of details. There are names of cities, of people involved, and of rulers; there are details regarding the timing of the event, and other pieces of information one would expect from a truthful testimony.

Lack of motive for fabrication:

Neither you nor I have any evidence to believe that the story of Angie's death is being fabricated. I have no reason to believe that someone would call me and claim to be a medical examiner and tell me my sister had died when she had not. Further, there is no reason to believe my wife made up the story about seeing Angie's hand. It would be hard for you to make the case that I am making this story up right now. I suppose that you could say that I am creating this to use it as an illustration, but that would require a greater leap of faith than believing that it is true.

Everyone knows that motive provides a great deal of circumstantial evidence for things. When it comes to the resurrection of Christ, to claim that those who testified about the resurrection made it up, we would have to propose some sort of motive for fabrication. This begs the question, "Why would they make up such a story?" Almost always, motives for fabrication involve some sort of personal gain. But it is very difficult to find a motive for fabrication among those who claimed Christ rose. They did not become rich. We don't know of any issues of prideful revenge. And, *in their lives*, they did not win any popularity contests. In fact, it would seem that most of them died a martyr's death. Even the Gospel writers did not include their names in their Gospels, showing us that they were not seeking fame. I am sure that we could come up with some theories for fabrication, but these theories require a great deal of *blind* faith to believe.

Incidental and obscure details:

When I told the story about Angie, I provided many details that were unnecessary. I told you about the conversation I had with the medical examiner word-for-word as I remember it. I told you that I was on Hwy 635. I told you a rather irrelevant story about how I thought it might have been a police officer calling me to pull me over. I told you that Angie's remains were in a plain white cardboard box. And I told you about how I almost went into the medical examiner's office to look at the pictures until he advised me not to.

A good indication that a story is true is when there are details told that are not necessarily relevant to the big picture. Sometimes these details will be confusing for the listener, but make sense for the one who is telling the story. When people are making stories up, they normally only include what is relevant to ensure the substance of the fabrication. In the accounts of Christ's life and resurrection, the Gospel writers include many details that are somewhat irrelevant from the standpoint of the hearer. For example, in John's Gospel, we are told that "the one whom Jesus loved" (John the writer of the book) outran Peter to the tomb (John 20:4). This information is completely irrelevant from the standpoint of the bigger story, but is a mark of the historicity of the events.

An example of a confusing detail is when Christ talked about the "unforgivable sin" (Matt. 12:32). Outside of Matthew and Luke, this idea is not spoken of again. It is not a theme of the Gospels and does not get explained later on. All of church history has been confused about what the "unforgivable sin" is. Most, like myself, would say that it amounts to a rejection of the Gospel. Either way, this is a mark of genuineness due to its obscure nature. When people are making stuff up, they normally make sure that *every* detail fits into the big picture of the fabrication and is easily understood.

I have just scratched the surface of the evidences for Christ's resurrection. My hopes are that by reading this small bit of evidence for the resurrection and comparing it to the evidence for my sister's death, you will see that we have valid reasons to believe both.

Let me ask you a question: Based on what you have read here, do you believe my sister Angie died in 2004? I imagine you do. Why? Because you, on autopilot, did not even need for me to explain the reasons why you were convicted that I was telling the truth. You were automatically filtering this through your already existing ability to test truth claims. In the end, you trust my testimony.

But you know what? While I think that the evidence here is substantial for us to believe that my sister died, I think that it is even more substantial for a belief in the resurrection of Christ. The reason why we don't often see it as such is because of the miraculous nature of the resurrection. People die every day. We experience it. People don't rise from the grave every day. I imagine none of you have experienced a resurrection. I understand this, but we must be careful. Our conviction cannot be forced through a presupposition that people cannot rise from the dead because we have not personally experienced it. That is what we call "question begging." It is assuming the conclusion (people cannot rise) and basing the way we look at the evidence upon this assumption (therefore, *whatever* the evidence says, it cannot say that Christ rose). We have to let the evidence itself produce a conclusion, not the other way around.

For some people this type of evidence will not be so important. I encourage you, whether this is what you *think* you need or not, to explore and examine the evidence for Christianity, specifically Christ's resurrection. I think you will find that while your belief that my sister died in 2004 can be strong, a belief in Christ's resurrection can be even stronger.

Discussion Questions:

1. Fill in your conviction meter chart. How high is the "forensic" sub-meter? Explain where you are at and why.

2. How important is this type of evidence for your faith? Explain.

3. Do you think that Christianity is seen by the outside world as a belief that has its forensic meter set a zero? Why or why not.

4. Do you believe that Angie died in 2004? Why or why not? How strong is your conviction?

5. Do you believe that Christ rose from the grave? What "footprints" or "finger prints" would you expect to find if such a monumental event actually occurred?

Keeping the Big Picture:

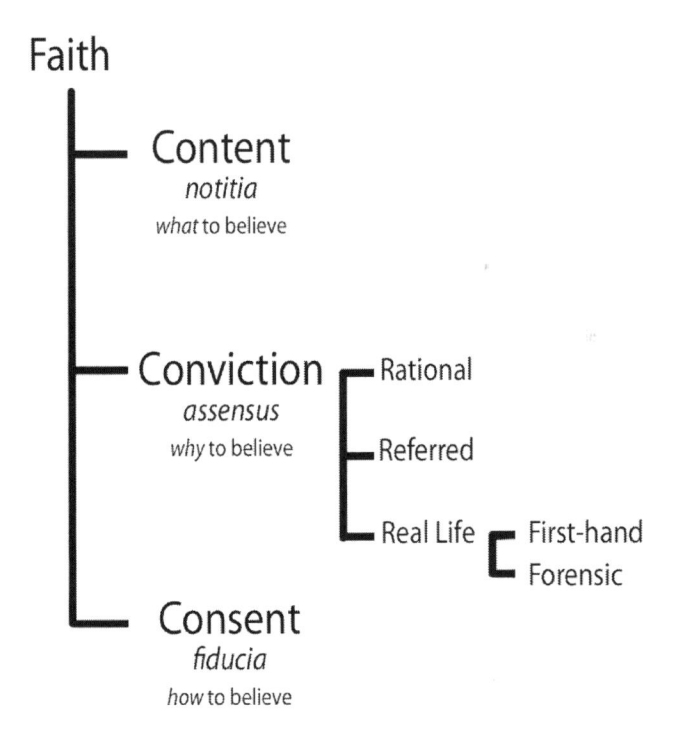

Faith
- **Content**
  notitia
  what to believe
- **Conviction**
  assensus
  why to believe
  - Rational
  - Referred
  - Real Life
    - First-hand
    - Forensic
- **Consent**
  fiducia
  how to believe

CHAPTER #10

FAITH IS A DECISION

One of my favorite books to give people who are considering marriage is titled *Love is a Decision* by Gary Smalley. It does a wonderful job of helping people graduate from the idea that love is something you "fall" into or is controlled by the volatility of emotions. Love is not a feeling; it is a decision we have to make every day. In marriage, this involves commitment and will. Each day we wake up and *decide* to love our spouses, not because it comes so easily as they beguile us with their irresistible beauty and charm, but because we act. We must decide each day to put the needs of another before our own. We must decide to bend our natural inclination towards self-serving in favor of serving the other. Our actions must be present, or there is no love. Why? Because love is a decision that involves acts of the will.

When it comes to our faith, we find parallels here. In fact, Christ taught this very principle when he said, "If you love me, you will keep my commandments" (John 14:15). The Christian faith is not one that is purely informational or intellectual. Of course, we have argued that information and intellect make up important components of our faith, but without love, faith is worthless. The type of

CHAPTER 10: FAITH IS A DECISION

faith to which Christ calls us is a faith that issues forth in love. And the kind of love Christ is calling us to is a love that acts.

The final aspect of Christian faith is called consent (*fiducia*).

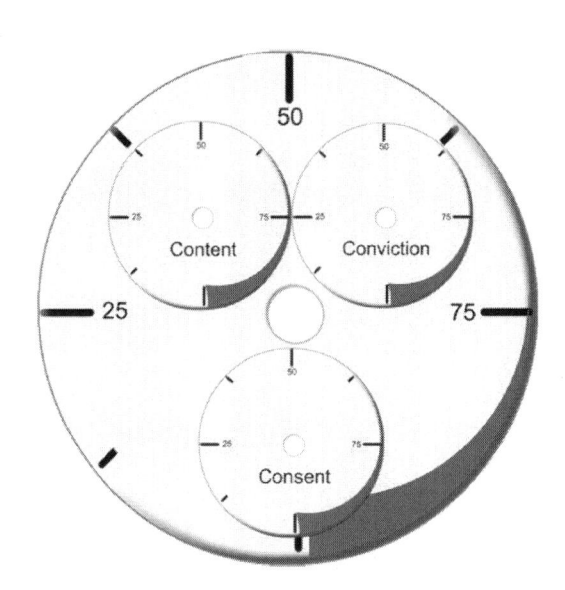

Without consent, one can have all the right information and even be fully convicted of its truthfulness, yet have no biblical faith whatsoever. While faith without content is problematic, and faith without conviction is weak, I believe faith without consent is the biggest problem the twenty-first century church faces. Dare I say, it could even be the biggest issue with *your* faith and the reason you are reading this book.

Consent speaks to acts of the will. To concede to something is to act in accordance with what you know to be true. It carries the idea of obedience, submission, and yielding. It is a decision. At some point, your faith must graduate into a decision.

The Chair

To illustrate what consent looks like, let me use a chair.

Suppose you came into my classroom one day and this chair was waiting for you. However, you don't like blind leaps of faith, so you take a few slow steps toward it. Noticing that you look a bit skeptical, I tell you that this is your chair. It has a seat, back, and four legs. This is the very definition of a chair. Thus far, I have given you the content of your faith. I have told you some basic facts as I understand them.

Next, you begin to examine the chair. You turn it over and check the manufacturer. You research the company on the internet and Consumer Reports, and find that it has a solid reputation of making safe chairs. You check all the screws and find that they are secure. You are feeling pretty confident not only that this is a chair, but that it can hold you if you sit down in it. However, you continue to test the chair. You have everyone in the class come and sit down in the chair to test its stability. It holds up perfectly. The content of your faith now has conviction added to it. You are convinced that the chair will hold you up.

However, suppose you did not take the next step. Suppose that instead of sitting down, you stood by the chair all day explaining to others how strong the chair was. Suppose you became an advocate for the integrity of the chair. Suppose you made flyers that summarized all the information you had researched, along with statistics, the history of the manufacturer, and testimonies from people who sat in the chair. You gave these flyers to anyone who passed by. Using our meter, this is what your faith in the chair would look like:

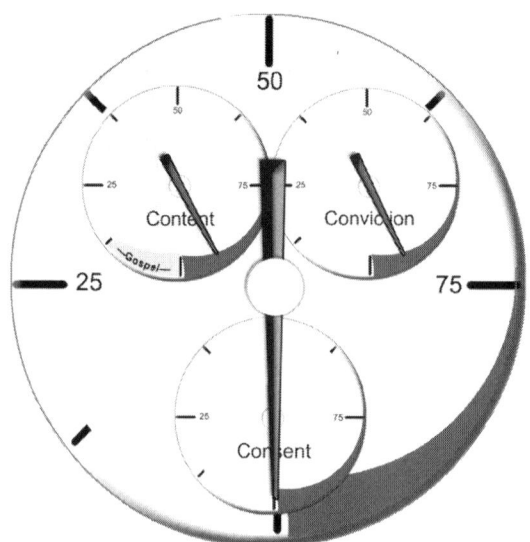

Notice that the content and conviction meter are high. These represent your knowledge about the chair, and your intellectual conviction that the chair is indeed trustworthy. However, the main faith meter has not moved at all. Your overall faith in the chair remains at zero. Why? Well, it is hard to see here, but the consent meter has not moved. You may say you believe in the chair and even tell others about how trustworthy the chair is, but you have never actually sat down in it yourself. You have not consented to your conviction. You have no true faith.

Many times, this is the problem with our faith. We live our lives thinking we believe, but not really believing. We have the right content and conviction, but we have never submitted our lives to the truth. I find this a lot in the so-called "Bible Belt". Growing up in Oklahoma, we have a lot of people with "Country Music" type of faith. You know what happens when you play a country music song backwards? You sober up, get back with your wife, and get both your dog and truck back! But playing forward, it is full of loss, heartbreak, broken relationships, and sin. However, there is no lack of talk about the Bible, God, or the "blood of the Lamb". There is lots of talk and real life (as Bono says "the 'stuff' of country songs); but no life change and real trust in God. Lots of content and conviction; no consent.

Faith of Demons

Think about it. Demons have the right content. They are even convicted of the truthfulness of the content. Yet their greatest flaw is a lack of consent. Notice what James has to say about this:

James 2:19
You believe that there is one God. Good! Even the demons believe that – and shudder.

In the context, James is dealing with a bunch of guys who say they have faith, but do not act upon this faith. They are selfish, prideful, and arrogant. They put up a banner called "Christian" outside their home, but their home life is far from Christ. They have a demon-type faith. They have yet to sit down in the chair.

James goes on to say something scathing to those of us who are Protestants:

James 2:24
You see that a person is justified by what he does and not by faith alone.

I am a Protestant. I believe that salvation comes by faith *alone*. In other words, I don't believe that there is anything you can *do* to earn favor before a perfect and just God. Our works are like filthy rags (Isaiah 64:6). Paul could not have put it more clearly:

Romans 11:6
And if [salvation is] by grace, then it is no longer by works; if it were, grace would no longer be grace.

Grace is a gift. In fact, the words grace and gift are taken from the same Greek root. You don't pay for a gift. You don't work for a gift. You don't strive for a gift. You don't beg for a gift. What if you received a Christmas gift from your mother, and immediately upon receiving it, you went upstairs, broke open your piggy bank, came back downstairs, and asked, "Oh, thank you. Now, how much do I owe you?" Your mother would rightly inform you that a gift cannot be paid for. It is not something you put on a payment plan, on layaway, or on a credit card. It is free. That is why it is called a gift. And that is why the grace of God cannot be earned.

So what does James mean when he says that a person is justified by "what he does"? In essence, he is saying what Protestants have said for a long time: "It is faith alone that saves, but the faith that saves will not be alone." In other words, James is coming down hard on the recipients of his letter for their failure to have the right *type* of faith. They loved the chair, thought the chair could hold anyone up, but were not actually sitting in the chair! They had no consent.

Often times we have the faith of demons, and we need to look this reality in the eye. If you live in America it is easy to call yourself Christian. It is easy to say you have faith in Christ. It is easy to say you believe in the resurrection. It is easy to go to church. It is easy to celebrate Christ's birth. It is easy to pray before meals. It is easy to go through all the motions, yet never really sit down. Faith is a decision that issues forth in action.

Two Sons

Christ told a parable about two sons:

Matthew 21:28-31
But what do you think? A man had two sons, and he came to the first and said, 'Son, go work today in the vineyard.' 29 "And he answered, 'I will not'; but afterward he regretted it and went. 30 "The man came to the second and said the same thing; and he answered, 'I will, sir'; but he did not go. 31 "Which of the two did the will of his father?" They said, "The first." Jesus said to them, "Truly I say to you that the tax collectors and prostitutes will get into the kingdom of God before you.

Notice here that the second son had a confession of faith and obedience. You could put it on a bumper sticker on the back of his car: "Dad said it, I believe it, that settles it." I bet there were bystanders applauding the second son's willingness and obedience. He said he would obey his dad without an argument. "A world-class boy you have there," they might have said. "I wish my children were so respectful." The son was probably swelling up with pride. *They are right on target, he thought to himself. I am a good son. I do love my dad. That bumper sticker on my car is well placed.*

But he did not obey. Oh, I imagine he had every intent to obey. However, other things came up. Maybe it was a baseball game. Maybe it was friends who came over with a case of beer. Maybe he just got tired and decided he would wait until tomorrow. Whatever the case, life interrupted his obedience and faith. What dad said, along with his initial commitment to obey, took second place to whatever came up.

On the other hand, the first son *seemed* like the rebellious one. "I will not." This is what he told his dad. No "maybe," no "If I get time," no "If my brother does, I will" – no contingency whatsoever. He was not going to obey. I can hear the bystanders this time, "What a rebellious child." "Someone ought to take him out to the wood shed." However, the first son changed. As other duties of the day began to fight for his allegiance, he had this nagging in the back of his mind. *He is my father. He is right. It is better to obey than not to obey.* Finally, he grabbed his shovel and went to work. Or, to continue our earlier analogy, the first son sat in the chair.

It is not our *confession* that reveals our faith, but our actions. At some point our faith has to start picking up shovels, sitting down in chairs, and believing in God rather than in ourselves.

Act of the Will

Remember, we are not called believers because we believed (past tense), but because we believe (present tense). God has introduced himself to us and offered salvation through Jesus Christ. He tells us to believe him. He says that he, being the creator of the world, knows what he is talking about. He says that his ways are not our ways, but that his ways are infinitely better than our ways:

Isa 55:8-9
For My thoughts are not your thoughts, nor are your ways My ways," declares the LORD. 9 "For as the heavens are higher than the earth, so are My ways higher than your ways and My thoughts than your thoughts.

He says there is going to be a way that seems right to us, but is not right. In fact, it ends up in death:

Pro 14:12
There is a way which seems right to a man, but its end is the way of death.

The question is, do we believe him? Are we ready to concede our way to his?

God opens our hearts to believe and we become believers: those who are characterized by our belief. Therefore, when God says that in him there is life and life more abundant (John 10:10), we show our trust in him by devoting ourselves to him. When we fail to devote ourselves to him, it may not be because we lack conviction of his trustworthiness, but simply because we refuse to concede our will to his. When he tells us it is better to refrain from sex before marriage, if we *truly* believe him, we consent. When he tells us that sobriety provides a better life and that in drunkenness there is destruction, we believe him and submit to his wisdom. When he tells us that it is better to give than to receive, we believe him and our checkbooks reflect it. When he says that the suffering of this present life is nothing to be compared to the glory that is coming, we trust him and endure the suffering with obedience. We don't seek for an escape. We are believers (present tense).

The final step to belief is an act of the will. It is not simply being fond of the Lord. It is not having an emotional attachment to him. It is not invoking his name into a conversation here and there. It is a life of utter dependence upon him. If we love him, we will do what he says.

Problem with the Will

However, like with the other components of faith, none of our consent meters are perfect. In fact, I would assume that even the best Christians fall short here. We are sinners. We still have a sinful bent in us called the "flesh." The flesh bends our will and causes us to not act in accordance with what it means to believe. When faced with a temptation, our will is often weak and we do things we don't want to do. Here is how the great Apostle Paul put it:

Romans 7:14-15
For we know that the Law is spiritual, but I am of flesh, sold into bondage to sin. 15 For what I am doing, I do not understand; for I am not practicing what I would like to do, but I am doing the very thing I hate.

We are often like Paul. While this is not the ideal life for a Christian, Paul is introducing us to the stark reality that our will is in a battle and it often loses. This is where faith takes on a very spiritual element. We know what is right and we know that the chair can hold us; we just can't seem to sit down consistently. At this point, our faith meter might look like this:

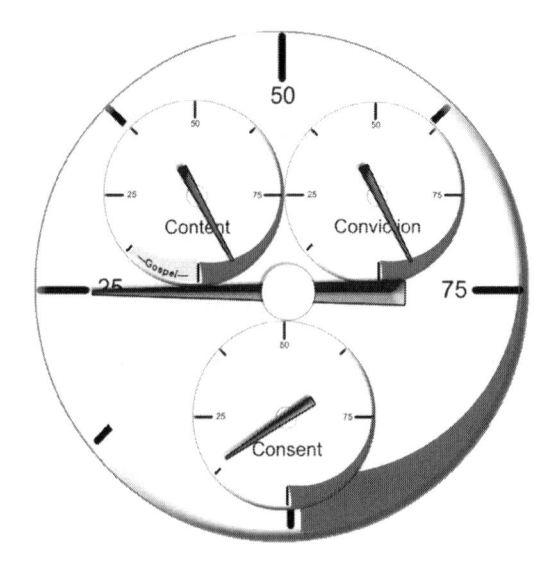

While the content and conviction is strong, the consent is lacking. This makes our overall faith weak. We have enough consent to rest in Christ for our salvation, but we lack the consent to actually live for him consistently. Our will is in the driver's seat of the car of life, while God is more like a back seat driver. He does just enough to make us feel guilty for the wrong turns, but not enough to get us out of the driver's seat. This is a dangerous place to be.

The Danger of Disobedience

Disobedience is addicting. Of course we are all going to be sinners for the rest of our lives. We are all going to fail until the day we die. The person who says he is not a sinner is under a delusion of the worst kind. John puts it this way:

1 John 1:8
If we say that we have no sin, we are deceiving ourselves and the truth is not in us.

But, thankfully, he follows it up with this:

1 John 1:9
If we confess our sins, he is faithful and just to forgive us our sins and

cleanse us from all unrighteousness.

Crossing the line of disobedience consistently will tear apart every aspect of our faith. Once that line is crossed, it gets easier and easier to cross it again. What we have to understand is that when God says to do something and we decide not to, it becomes habit. Sure, as Paul said earlier, we don't want to disobey, but we do; worse yet, we find a thousand and one ways to justify it.

"My anger outbursts may be bad, but at least they are not as bad as *his*."

"I am entitled to spend this money on myself. After all, look how hard I worked."

"I made all the right decisions. I deserve to think more highly of myself than I do of *that* person, who can't get it right."

"Why should I share? This is a tough world. Either eat or get eaten."

"You don't buy a car before you test drive it. Why shouldn't I live with my girlfriend before marrying her?"

"After all I have been through, I deserve to get drunk."

"So many bad things have happened to me, I have the right to worry."

These types of justifications for our sin are a reflection of our humanity. They are emblematic of the flesh. We will hear this type of rationale (from the devil on our shoulders) until the day we die. But knowing what is right and not doing it is destructive to every aspect of who we are. Justifying our sin leads to further disobedience and ultimately a loss of our faith. Some of you reading this are suffering significant doubt because you are disobeying regularly and justifying your disobedience in one way or another.

James tells us that when we know what God says but do not act accordingly, we are in danger of having our faith paralyzed.

James 1:22-24
But prove yourselves doers of the word, and not merely hearers who delude themselves. 23 For if anyone is a hearer of the word and not a doer, he is like a man who looks at his natural face in a mirror; 24 for once he has looked at himself and gone away, he has immediately forgotten what kind of person he was.

This tells us that there will be a battle within us for our whole lives; we will be fighting to graduate from hearing God's truth to doing God's truth. But when we don't obey – when we don't change the problems we see in the mirror – we will develop a condition of toxic disobedience.

Christ told a parable that many of you are familiar with. It is often called "The Parable of the Seeds," but should probably be titled "The Parable of the Soils." It appears in Luke 8:5-18. In essence, we have the seed, which is the word of God, and the soil, which is our heart. The seed is spread liberally. Some of the seed falls on the path, and Satan picks it up before it can take root. This reflects a person who did not believe at all. Other seed falls among rocks, where it finds some root, but due to the persecution involved with following Christ, it eventually dies. Other seed falls among the thorns. This seed finds root for a time, but dies as well, due to prioritization of the things the world has to offer over caring for the nascent faith. Finally, there is the last type of seed. It falls among good soil, takes root, and bears fruit that lasts.

Unfortunately, many people see this parable only in regards to one's salvation. In truth, it is written to both believers and unbelievers. It illustrates the way we believe. The soil of our heart must be prepared. Every time God speaks, his "seed" falls on one of these four types of soils. True faith is represented only by the soil that is not mindful of persecutions or worldly pleasure.

But this is not why I include this parable in this chapter. What comes next is the most telling and the most important part of the story. Christ concludes the parable this way:

Luke 8:18
So take care how you listen; for whoever has, to him more shall be given; and whoever does not have, even what he thinks he has shall be taken away from him.

Notice here he says take care *how* you listen. This is very interesting. The parable is not concerned with "what" we listen to. We already know it is the word of God. The issue is "how" we listen. If we listen to God's word and are not prepared to obey, it would be better off if we did not listen at all. Christ says that the one who has shall be given more. What does that mean? It means that the one who listens and obeys will be given more. More what? More faith. That is the subject: *how* we believe. But when we don't obey, even what we have will be taken away. So what will be taken away? Our faith. In other words, when we build a habit of hearing God but not obeying God, our faith will turn into doubt and shipwreck our life. The faith that we had will be taken away.

I come across people all the time who wonder why their faith is failing. They wonder why they doubt so much. More often than not, there is disobedience in their lives. They have known what God's will is yet consistently turned their backs on him, rationalizing their disobedience. I have been there myself many times. In the country of disobedience, faith is no resident. Once this becomes a pattern, even what you have, your content and conviction, will be taken away.

If your faith is suffering significantly, if you conviction is not so strong anymore, if doubts have infested your reading of God's word, there may be a pattern of disobedience that has taken hold in your life. The solution is terribly difficult and terribly simple at the same time: obey. Build patterns of obedience. Make a commitment to act upon everything God says. When you fail, don't rationalize it. Ask for forgiveness, pick yourself back up, and try again. If you fail a thousand times (which – join the club – you may), pick yourself up a thousand and one times. Don't ever settle for rationalized disobedience. Faith is a decision.

Trusting in Christ for salvation involves resting in him like you rest in a chair. It is a turn from self-reliance to Christ-reliance. Thus begins the Christian life of faith. But it does not end there. We count God as the most reliable being in the universe. He knows what we don't. Yes, he lays down rules. Yes, he demands everything. Yes, he calls on us to sacrifice. Yes, he tells us doing what is right is better than having fun. But he is not a cosmic killjoy. He does know what he is talking about. Rest in him. Sit down in the chair. It really is trustworthy. God is pretty smart.

Discussion Questions:

1. Do you think that the church today is suffering from low consent meter?

2. How would you rate yourself on the consent meter?

3. In what ways have you failed to sit down in the chair even though you know it is trustworthy?

4. Names some instances where you have rationalized disobedience.

5. Do you ever feel as if the faith you have is being taken away from you? Explain. What is the solution?

Keeping the Big Picture:

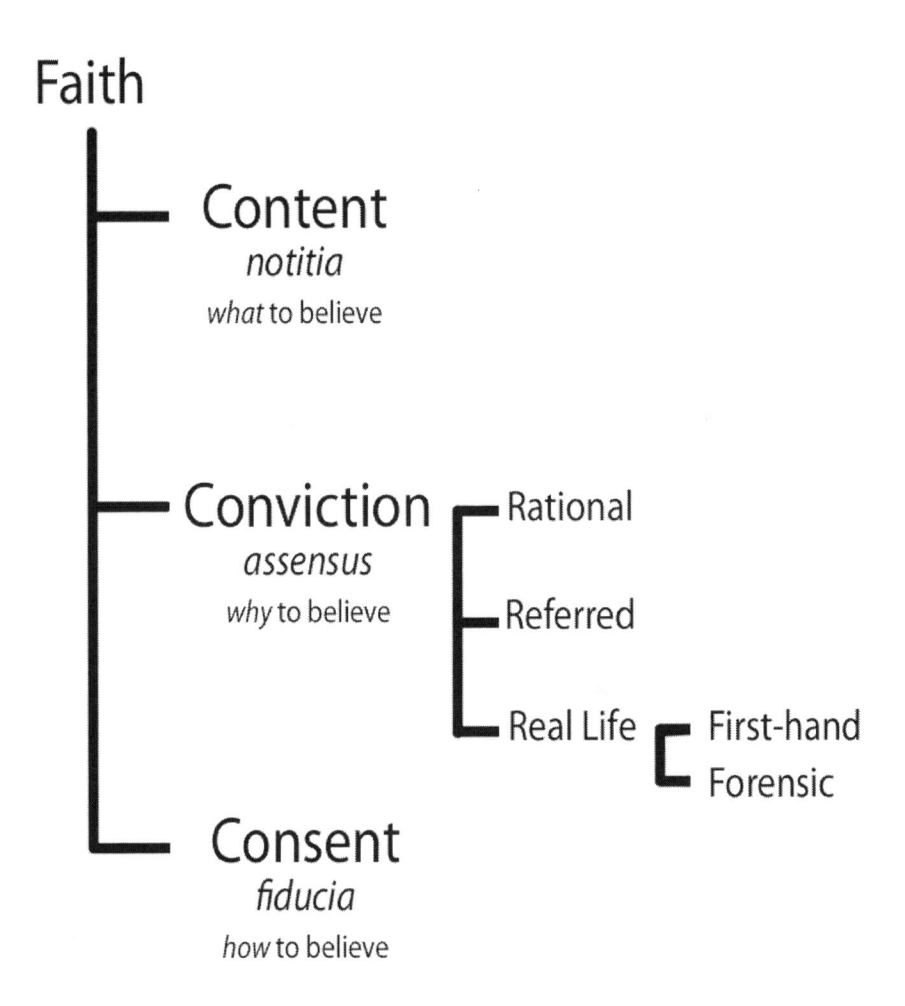

Faith

- **Content**
  notitia
  what to believe

- **Conviction** — Rational
  assensus
  why to believe — Referred

  — Real Life — First-hand
  — Forensic

- **Consent**
  fiducia
  how to believe

CHAPTER #11

FIXING OUR FAITH

Many of us find ourselves battling for our faith. Others are content with a minimalist faith. Some just don't want to make it too complicated. Yet faith is the foundation of the Christian life. If we don't know *how* to believe, *what* we believe will suffer greatly. What I have presented in this book is not rocket science. It is not solely for the seminarian. It is not for those who have been Christians for a long time. This is discipleship 101.

Whether your faith is suffering from a lack of content, conviction, or consent, there are steps to take to make things right. Let me share a few with you.

For Those Who Lack Content

The content of our faith has a primary source, which serves as its ultimate authority. Neither our opinions, nor our experiences, nor our feelings, nor our friends should take center stage, not even the pastor of your church. It is the Bible. Scripture is our authority. Though God guides and directs our steps in many ways through our reason, experiences, emotions, and influences, these all take a backseat to the

CHAPTER 11: FIXING OUR FAITH

Bible. The Bible is God's word. Jesus Christ is the ultimate content of our faith, but it is through the Scriptures that we learn of him and he speaks to us.

For some of you the solution to your ailing faith is simple. We sometimes call this "getting into the Word." I don't like clichés, but this one will have to do. *Get into the Word of God!* This is one of the most important disciplines in the Christian life. In order to communicate its importance, God called on the Israelites to dwell upon his words morning, day, and night. He even used hyperbole, saying that they should tattoo his words on their foreheads!

Deuteronomy 6:6-9
And these words, which I am commanding you today, shall be on your heart; 7 and you shall teach them diligently to your sons and shall talk of them when you sit in your house and when you walk by the way and when you lie down and when you rise up. 8 And you shall bind them as a sign on your hand and they shall be as frontals on your forehead. 9 And you shall write them on the doorposts of your house and on your gates.

Knowing God's word is not of minimal importance. It is the *sine qua non* ("without which, nothing") of faith. This does not mean you simply go to a good church that preaches and teaches from God's word (as important as that is); you must continually read and dwell upon the Bible *yourself*.

The biggest excuse I hear from people about reading the Bible is that they don't understand it. Granted, much of it is hard to understand, but most of the time those who say this are simply rationalizing their lack of faith. However, I rarely meet someone who truly wants to grow in her faith that makes this excuse. This does not mean our desire to grow makes everything in the Bible clear, but it does add the element of desire to the reading. Once this is present, we are constantly asking ourselves "What does this mean? What does this say about God? What does it say about me? What does God want me to know through this?" Once these questions are asked, the Bible becomes a treasure chest of relevant content.

However, as many of you know, people who read and study the Bible *still* can be plagued with corrupted content. And if your content is bad, it does not matter how convicted you are of its truthfulness and it does not matter how much you concede to its words. If it is wrong content, then it is wrong faith.

Therefore, we must read and study the Bible the right way. Every Christian needs to learn proper methods of Biblical interpretation. The Bible is not a magic book. You cannot open it up, point to a verse, and get God's direction for the day. It does not work that way. It is an ancient collection of sixty-six books, written by over forty authors over a span of fifteen hundred years. The latest book is nearly two thousand years old. There are dozens of different genres of literature contained within it, and each genre communicates truths in different ways. There are histories, biographies, laments, songbooks, and highly symbolic prophecies. Bible study is a discipline. Yes, it will take some work. It will take some *hard* work. But it is not beyond your reach. We spend nearly twenty years of our lives receiving education in school. Then we go to our jobs and are trained for months about details of our industry. We never cease to learn. Is it too hard to devote ourselves to becoming students of the information that the God of our universe has said is *most* important?

Appendix A discusses an excellent method for studying the Bible. It will serve as a helpful guide to get you to the next step in your Bible study.

"But there are too many interpretations!" someone objects. Yes, it is true that there are many interpretations out there. But what I have found is that when people study the Bible properly, using the method I have provided, there are not *that* many interpretations, especially about the main issues. The many interpretations only come when people see the Bible as a magic book that has no rules of interpretation. When the rules are followed, the number of possible interpretations decreases dramatically.

Read your Bible. Study your Bible. Take a course on how to interpret the Bible. Find a good church that teaches the Bible. Find a study group to discuss the Bible. Dwell on the Bible. Memorize the Bible. God does not speak in vain. The Bible is not optional to our faith. Its message is our faith's foundation.

For Those Who Lack Conviction

I received a call not too long ago from a young man who wanted my help. He said that he had been a Christian all his life, but he was losing his faith. Like with the pastor I spoke of earlier, the most significant part of the conversation was when he pleaded with me for help, saying, "I want to believe! I want my faith back." After weeks of conversation through emails and phone calls, the problem with his faith became apparent. Through all the years of being a "Christian," he was never really convicted of the truthfulness of what he professed. He went through the motions, acted in accordance with his professed beliefs, taught Sunday school every week, encouraged his kids to read their Bible, and even exhorted other people to believe. Unfortunately, he never realized that he did not *really* believe himself. All of his content was good. Consent was definitely present. But he did not have any real conviction to stabilize his faith – it was completely blind. It was not unlike a faith in Santa Claus or the Tooth Fairy. He inherited it from his parents, and this alone was his foundation. But God has no grandchildren. Our faith must be our own.

Many of you reading this have never thought of faith as something that can be rational. It has never crossed your mind that there could actually be evidence for your belief in God. Until now, you viewed faith as a blind leap into the dark. But God does not want you to remain here.

There are many problems people have that disturb their faith. Here are some of the most common:

The silence of God

Why doesn't God reveal himself more clearly through ordinary means of communication? More simply, why doesn't God talk, and why can't we see him? As my son Zach said, when he was four and I was telling him about God, "Where is he? I can't see him."

Contradictions in the Bible

Why does the Bible say that we are not to murder, but God sanctions the killing of all the Canaanites? Why does it say that there were two angels at the tomb in one Gospel, and only one in another?

Hell

Why does God say he loves everyone, yet sends some of those he loves to hell to suffer for all eternity?

Evolution

Doesn't evolution prove that God does not exist and that the Bible is wrong about creation?

Miracles

How am I supposed to believe that snakes talked, seas parted, the blind were healed, and people who were swallowed by whales survived? Sound more like myth than history. I never see that kind of stuff.

Suffering

How could a good God allow so much evil and tragedy in a world he loves? There are dozens more. Maybe I have represented your difficulties and maybe I have not. However, these are issues that disrupt intellectual conviction for many.

The first thing we must realize is that no question you could ever pose is new. I think this is important to realize. When I first started asking these questions, my biggest fear was that I was the only one who was even raising my hand with the red flag. I feared asking these questions because I thought they could prove to be the undoing of my faith, and I did not want

CHAPTER 11: FIXING OUR FAITH

that. However, we must realize we are not that smart, and other Christians are not that dumb. For two thousand years, great Christians have addressed these issues and remained strong in their faith. Why? Because these questions *do* have answers.

The second thing we must realize is that God is not afraid of our questions. He is not in heaven speaking to the other members of the Trinity saying, "Oh no. Michael just asked about the apparent contradiction in the resurrection story. Now I am going to damn him to hell for all eternity." God does not mind our inquiry. In fact, as I showed in the chapter on rational conviction, he calls on us to use our heads. He is not fond of blind and irrational faith (to put it mildly).

The third thing we must realize is that we don't have to have all our questions answered in order to believe. Whenever I have contact with someone whose faith is suffering due to their lack of intellectual conviction in one or more areas, I normally don't start with the issue that is causing distress. I deal with two things: 1) The existence of God and 2) the historicity of the resurrection of Christ. Once you are stabilized in your conviction that God exists, you can grasp that his presence in this world is evidenced through the resurrection of Christ. It is a one-two punch of apologetics.

Concerning the existence of God, I encourage readers to study the arguments for his existence. Appendix B can help get you started. I believe you will find that for all its claims to the contrary, atheism (the denial of God's existence) is also a type of faith whose doctrines are completely bankrupt when it comes to intellectual vitality. In other words, atheism is about the blindest leap of faith a person can take.

After stabilizing your faith in the existence of God, I would encourage you to look into the historicity of Christ's resurrection. You see, once you are convinced that Christ rose from the grave, the implications are tremendous. Rarely have I met a Christian who had strong conviction about Christ's resurrection, yet was having faith-threatening problems with God's silence, the problem of suffering, or evolution. If Christ has risen from the grave,

Christianity is true. Period. If he has not risen from the grave, Christianity is false. Period. Don't take my word for it, listen to Paul:

1 Corinthians 15:13-14
"But if there is no resurrection of the dead, not even Christ has been raised; 14 and if Christ has not been raised, then our preaching is vain, your faith also is vain.

I can't intellectually defend the historicity of a donkey talking or Samson's super-human strength. But I don't have to. You see, there are two things God has called people to look at when his reality is at stake. In the Old Testament he was continually pointing the wavering Israelites to look back to the Exodus. In the New Testament we are encouraged to look at the Resurrection of Christ.

Appendix C contains a brief defense of Christ's resurrection to get you started.

Issues with Consent

Remember the story about the doctor I was witnessing to in the consent chapter? The "someday, maybe…" guy? For some of us, that is where we are. "Someday, maybe…" is our response too. We are always one question away from making the decision to trust him. I am not saying there are not legitimate questions that we need answered. What I am saying is that at some point, our indecisiveness becomes a definite decision. Our lack of faith in Christ is our new blind faith.

Our conviction does not need to be perfect before we rest in Christ. It just needs to be true and sufficient.

Others of us have simply built a habit of disobedience. We develop patterns in our brain which make disobeying the eternal creator no big deal. We rationalize, believing that his grace will cover us. Due to the lack of immediate consequences for many of our sins, we start to think that God is winking his eye at our wrong turns. We begin to forget, it is these things that sent Christ to the cross.

Yes, when you have trusted in Christ, you are saved. Nothing can change the fact that you are in God's family. But, no, God does not wink an eye at our sin. He is incredibly gracious and longsuffering, but there is a point where he will allow us to go into the destruction we seek through repeated disobedience. Like the Prodigal son, who left his father to go the way of the world, we set off on the journey to sin. What we may fail to realize is that his father let him go. The father let him suffer the consequences of sin and debauchery. God has set the world up in such a way that there *are* consequences for our sin. Some are immediate, while others take time to bear their fruit. But the Lord disciplines precisely because he wants our faith to be in him, not what the world has to offer. He reproves those whom he loves.

Revelation 3:19
Those whom I love, I reprove and discipline; be zealous therefore, and repent.

Paul compares our lack of consent to mocking God. When we don't act on what he says, it is like thumbing our noses at him.

Galatians 6:7
Do not be deceived, God is not mocked; for whatever a man sows, this he will also reap.

While God may not strike us with loving discipline every time we take a wrong turn (thank God), those wrong turns will add up. There is a reaping. And eventually, the lack of consent in our faith will harvest the terrible fruit of destruction. Sometimes this destruction is so bad that we cannot recover; sometimes there is recovery. This does not mean God no longer loves us. But it does mean that sometimes, he will let us go.

Again, we will never be perfect. But this fact does not give us a "hall pass" to mock God by hearing his word, being convicted of its truthfulness, yet not following what it says.

Faith is a Gift

Finally, we must always be mindful that faith is a gift. Better put, the ability to acquiesce our will to God's is nothing less than miracle. Every aspect of our faith is a gift from God. God did not have to give us the Scriptures (content). He did not have to create us with the ability to understand (conviction). And any time we actually sit down in the chair (consent) it is an act of our will, which has been empowered by the Holy Spirit.

Philippians 2:13
For it is God who is at work in you, both to will and to work for His good pleasure.

Notice here that God is the force behind our will and our ability to act according to our belief. He is the one who is working out the faith within us.

Ephesians 2:8
For by grace you have been saved through faith; and that not of yourselves, *it is* the gift of God.

The Greek construction here tells us the "that" in this sentence in inclusive of the entire salvation process. Everything, including faith, is a gift of God. He goes on:

Ephesians 2:9
Not as a result of works, so that no one may boast.

There is no boasting in heaven. God is very concerned that our faith be understood in such a way that we have only him to blame. God is the conductor of the orchestra of faith. What is the end goal of our faith? Consent, obedience, trust, sitting down in the chair, and getting our shovels. Notice here:

Ephesians 2:10
For we are His workmanship, created in Christ Jesus for good works, which God prepared beforehand so that *we would walk in them*. (emphasis mine)

Why all of this at the conclusion of this book? Because, in the end, we must know that we are completely at God's mercy. Every aspect of our faith is a gift. The increase of our faith comes only from him. God wants us to have the right knowledge. God wants us to become increasingly convicted of his trustworthiness. And God wants us to rest in him, trusting him to have the right map of this world. In short, as we began the book upon the foundation of love, God wants our faith to love him completely. The greatest commandment is to "Love the Lord with all your heart, with all your soul, and with all your mind" (Matthew 22:37). This cannot happen unless our faith is increased. Increase our faith, Lord.

APPENDIX A

HOW TO STUDY THE BIBLE IN A NUTSHELL

The following is a practical guide to biblical interpretation, which follows a three-step process I have used for years. The Bible is two thousand years old and often seems very archaic. This makes it hard to know how it applies to us. This can be very frustrating, as all Christians are encouraged to read their Bible daily but often are at a loss as to how to understand it and apply the message to their own lives. The process I will explain here has served me well; I believe it is the best way to interpret the ancient word of God and apply it today. I hope it will alleviate some of the "Bible interpretation anxiety" that is out there and allow the Bible to become real and relevant to your life and faith.

Notice the three sections of the chart (on next page). There are three audiences that Bible readers need to recognize in the process of interpreting the Bible. In the bottom left, you have the "ancient audience." This represents the original audience and the original author. The top portion represents the "timeless audience," which transcends the time and culture of the original situation. It is that which applies to all people in all places at all times, without regard to cultural and historical issues. Finally, we have the "contempo-

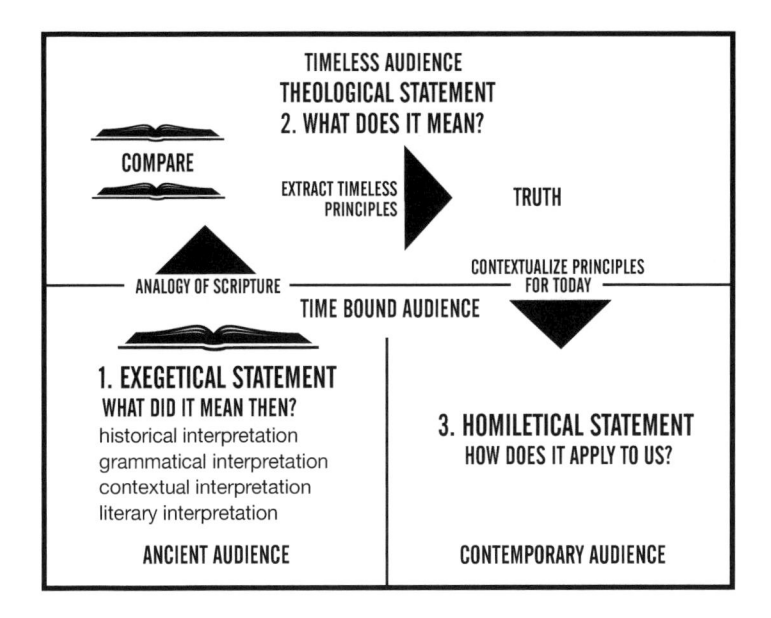

```
                    TIMELESS AUDIENCE
                 THEOLOGICAL STATEMENT
                   2. WHAT DOES IT MEAN?
    COMPARE
                 EXTRACT TIMELESS
                   PRINCIPLES          TRUTH

                              CONTEXTUALIZE PRINCIPLES
ANALOGY OF SCRIPTURE                FOR TODAY
                   TIME BOUND AUDIENCE

1. EXEGETICAL STATEMENT
WHAT DID IT MEAN THEN?
historical interpretation        3. HOMILETICAL STATEMENT
grammatical interpretation       HOW DOES IT APPLY TO US?
contextual interpretation
literary interpretation

    ANCIENT AUDIENCE             CONTEMPORARY AUDIENCE
```

rary audience" in the bottom right. This represents us, today. Here we will develop applications from the Bible that relate to our time, culture, and circumstances.

In Biblical interpretation, it is of extreme importance that one goes in the order of the chart. The goal is to find out *first* what the Bible meant, then what it means, and last, how it applies to us. So many people start with the third step, then fail miserably in understanding God's word. Others start with step number two, attempting to force their own theology on the text. It is important that all steps are covered in order to ensure interpretive fidelity.

Step one: Exegetical Statement

What did it mean then?

The first step is the most important. Here the goal is to ascertain the original intent of the writing. It is very important that one enters into the world of the author and the audience. Sometimes this will be easy; sometimes it will be very difficult, requiring quite a bit more study.

Here are the different issues you must consider:

Historical issues: Recognizing the historical circumstances will aid your understanding of the text. Here, you ask questions of occasion. Who is the original author? Who is the original audience? What purpose did the writing have? When Moses wrote the Pentateuch, what was his occasion or purpose? Was it to give an exhaustive history of the world to everyone, or to prepare the Israelite religious community to exist in a theocratic society under Yahweh? When Paul wrote his letter to the Corinthians, what was his purpose? Knowing that in 2 Corinthians he was writing to defend his apostleship, as other false apostles were opposing him, is essential to understanding every verse. As well, what was Paul's disposition toward the Galatians when he wrote to them? Was it to commend, condemn, or correct? The occasion will determine so much of our understanding.

Grammatical issues: It is important to understand that the Bible was written in different languages. The New Testament was written in Greek. Not only that, but it was a particular kind of Greek called "Koine", which is the dialect of Greek spread by Alexander the Great. Most of the Old Testament was written in Hebrew, with small portions in Aramaic. Naturally, other languages have ideas that communicate well in the original tongue but can get lost in translation. Greek words, for example, use inflections (word endings) which determine their part of speech. Word placement can add emphasis. These nuances are often hard to translate. I am not saying everyone needs to be a Greek and Hebrew scholar to understand the Bible; only that there are grammatical issues that can nuance our understanding of the passage. A good commentary will normally bring these to light.

Contextual issues: Every book was written for a purpose. The smallest component of a word is a letter. We don't take each letter in isolation, but understand that a group of letters makes a word. We don't take each word in isolation, understanding that a group of words makes a sentence. And we don't take sentences in isolation, understanding that a group of sentences

APPENDIX A: HOW TO STUDY THE BIBLE IN A NUTSHELL

makes a paragraph. But we don't stop there. Each paragraph is part of a larger whole, which we call a "pericope." The pericope is the basic argument or story that is being told. The story of David and Goliath is a pericope, told in many paragraphs. As well, Christ's parables make up individual pericopes. Finally, each pericope is a smaller part of an entire book. The purpose of the book will shape the context in which each pericope should be interpreted.

Here is how it looks:

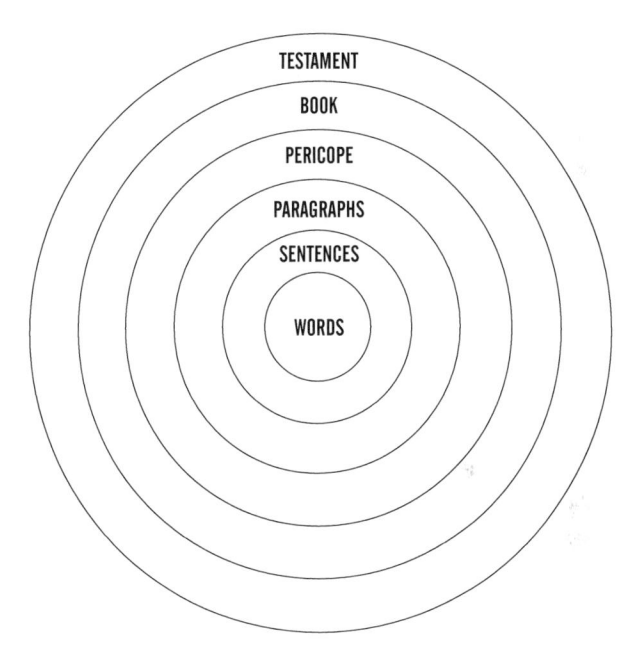

TESTAMENT
BOOK
PERICOPE
PARAGRAPHS
SENTENCES
WORDS

Literary issues: We must remember that there is no such type of literature called "Bible" or "Scripture." The Bible is made up of many books, from many different types of literature called "genres." Just like in your everyday life, you encounter many genres and know almost instinctively that they follow different rules of understanding. There are fictional novels, newspaper editorials, commercials, television dramas, academic textbooks, and tickers at the bottom of the news station. Each of these needs to be understood and interpreted according to the rules of its particular genre. In the Bible, we find narratives, histories, parables, apocalyptic prophecies, personal letters, public letters, songs, proverbs, and many others. Each of these must be interpreted according to the rules of its genre. Just because they are in the Bible does not mean the rules change. For example, a proverb is a common type of literature found in the Bible, but also in many other cultures. A proverb is a statement of general truth or wisdom that does not necessarily apply in every situation. A proverb is not a promise. If it is in the Bible, it is still not a promise. As well, theological histories are just that – theological. Being in the Bible does not magically make it a technically precise and exhaustive history that is supposed to answer every question that we have. We must determine the type of literature we are dealing with if we are to understand it.

Genesis, Exodus, Leviticus, Numbers, Deuteronomy, Joshua, Judges, Ruth, 1 Samuel, 2 Samuel, 1 Kings, 2 Kings, 1 Chronicles, 2 Chronicles, Ezra, Nehemiah, Esther	History/Narrative	To give a theological history of Isreal in narrative form
Psalms	Poetry	Emotional praises and cries to God
Job, Proverbs, Ecclesiastes, Song of Solomon	Wisdom	Instructions for wise living
Isaiah, Jeremiah, Lamentations, Ezekiel, Daniel, Hosea, Joel, Amos, Obadiah, Jonah, Micah, Nahum, Habakkuk, Zephaniah, Haggai, Zechariah, Malachi	Prophecy	Call Isreal to repentance
Matthew, Mark, Luke, John, Acts	History/Narrative	To give a theological history of Christ
Romans, 1 Corinthians, 2 Corinthians, Galatians, Ephesians, Philippians, Colossians, 1 Thessalonians, 2 Thessalonians, 1 Timothy, 2 TimothyTitus, Philemon, Hebrews, James, 1 John, 2 John, 3 John, Jude	Epistle	Didactic and Pastoral letters written to explain Theological teaching for the Church
Revelation	Apacolyptic	Message of hope for the Church

Step two: Theological Statement

What does it mean for all people in all places at all times?

Here is where you move from what was being said to what is always being said; from what was being taught to what is always being taught; from what the (original) author was saying to his audience to what the Author (God) is always saying to all people. The audience here is timeless and universal. You are extracting the timeless principles for all people, in all places, at all times.

Principle: A general truth that that applies universally. A doctrine. A fundamental law. The underlying reality. The essence of the action. The reason for the norm.

Sometimes it is very easy to find the principle, as there is no cultural baggage to extract or interpret. Other times, it can be very difficult. There are not always principles to universalize. More often than not, the text will only be communicating what was done in the past, without any mandate to follow the example. An easy illustration is when Paul told Timothy to bring him the cloak (coat) he left in Troas (2 Tim 4:13). This is not to be universalized in some way to mean Christians are supposed to continually be bringing each other coats, clothes, or any other articles of clothing. It is simply what Paul needed in his time, and we must allow it to be limited to such. Therefore, you must distinguish between what is prescribed and what is merely described.

On the other hand, we also have material that is already as a principle. For example, when the author of Hebrews says that Jesus Christ "will never leave you or forsake you" (Heb. 13:5), in the context, this is already a principle. In other words, there is no reason to think that he is only saying this to the recipients of the book in the sixties; there is every reason to believe this refers to all Christians of all times. We must simply ask if the passage applies universally or locally.

One way to determine this is to follow the analogy of Scripture shown on the original chart. Here you are to ask if the Bible, in other places, confirms, repeals, or denies the principle or action. For example, much of the Law in the Old Testament does not have any application to us today, either theologically or in practice. Why? Because Christ fulfilled the law in many ways. The New Testament explicitly tells us that we are not under the law. Therefore, when it comes to animal sacrifices, we no longer need to practice this in any way. Christ's sacrifice fulfilled this law.

At other times, principles will not be overshadowed by a fulfillment; often, they will be confirmed in multiple other places. This lets us know that the principle is universal, not limited to a particular moment in redemptive history. For example, the command not to commit adultery, first found in Exodus, is never repealed and is confirmed in many other places. This is the analogy of Scripture.

Once a solid interpretation has been made, one must look for reinforcement for the principle in other places. These places should never be thought of as more authoritative than Scripture itself, but as an interpretive aid in responsibly coming to a conclusion. Here are the four places to look:

Reason: Is the interpretation reasonable? Does it make sense? I am not talking here in a subjective sense, but in a very formal sense. If your interpretation directly conflicts with other known information, then the filter of reason will drive you back to Scripture to reassess your conclusion. Truth cannot contradict itself. The filter of reason will provide a valuable means of assessment concerning your interpretation.

Tradition: What do others say about it? Here, you will be dipping into the deep rich well of two-thousand years of church history asking for help. If we believe the Holy Spirit is in all Christians, we can find aid in the advice of the Spirit-led community. Not only should you look to contemporary scholars and theologians, but also to the history of the Church. What has the church said about this passage or issue throughout time? If you come to a different conclusion than the historic body of Christ, it is a good sign that you have taken a wrong interpretive turn somewhere (though this is

APPENDIX A: HOW TO STUDY THE BIBLE IN A NUTSHELL

not always the case).

Experience: Don't be surprised here. Albeit fallible, our experience is a very important interpretive guide. If your interpretation contradicts your experience, this could be a sign that your interpretation is wrong. For example, when we interpret Christ in the upper room discourse concerning prayer "in his name," we could get the idea that we can ask for anything in his name and expect to receive it. "Please give me a new 2010 Camaro, in Jesus' name." "Please heal my mother, in Jesus' name." "Please remove this depression, in Jesus' name." Been there, done that (remember my third year at the cakewalk?). We all have. When the magic formula does not correspond to our experience, we return to Scripture to search for other interpretive options, as well we should. God expects and requires the application of experience in our interpretation of Scripture. The Bible is impossible to understand without an assumption of experience. While experience can lead us wrong, and we don't believe that it can contradict rightly interpreted Scripture, it can help us figure out how to rightly interpret Scripture.

Emotion: Like with experience, we must be very careful here. Our emotions can be extremely important and also extremely misleading. First, they are important by analogy. When we read about God's love, in order for us to understand this love, we are expected to have some degree of the emotion ourselves. For us to know what "the peace that passes understanding" is, we have to have experienced some sort of peace in our lives. If we have not, our understanding is going to be two-dimensional. Second, our emotions can direct us to right understanding. We are told that the Holy Spirit convicts us of truth. This internal conviction must be a valid source of information. If we feel that an interpretation of a passage is wrong because it does not seem to be emotionally satisfying, this could be an indication that it is indeed wrong. Yet we must be careful here, as our emotions can also be guided by sinful elements, which can lead us to wrong interpretation. Nevertheless, it is a necessary part of the theological process to recognize the role our emotions play, both good and bad, in our understanding of Scripture. If we deny them, acting as if they have no part to play, we are only fooling ourselves.

Extraction of the Principles

Once your interpretation has been filtered and affirmed through these things, the cultural baggage must be completely extracted. Again, this involves separating the principles themselves from the ways in which they are applied in various contexts. The danger of skipping step two is tremendous. Skipping this step can make the Bible irrelevant if people fail to realize that there were cultural issues (at the time of the writing) that can determine a principle's application. These cultural issues are not timeless, and will have little relevance in other places. For example, Paul tells the Romans to "greet each other with a holy kiss." While the principle of showing affection transcends culture, if you don't extract that principle and apply it properly in your context, you might find yourself in a heap of trouble if you attempt to kiss someone who takes it the wrong way. Interpretation: the act of greeting someone with a kiss is not an acceptable way of showing affection in some cultures. Nowadays, a handshake is often sufficient. You cannot skip step two.

Another example: Paul speaks to the Corinthians of the necessity of women's head coverings. What we must ask ourselves is whether or not women wearing head coverings is an eternal requirement of God, or if the idea represents some underlying principle. When I was at church last week, most of the women there were not wearing hats, or any sort of covering at all. Does this mean that the women of this church do not believe or submit to Scripture? Doing a historical study of this issue reveals that head coverings, in Corinthian culture (as well as in many today), represented a woman's submission to her husband and her sexual modesty. In that culture, a woman's hair was a representation and revelation of her beauty. Failing to wear a head covering was sexually provocative in that culture. This has implications toward the marital bonds and fidelity. However, it is modesty and fidelity that are at issue, not simply wearing a hat. In this case, extracting the timeless principle means that the cultural baggage of expression – the hat – gets discarded so that the real issue can come into focus.

We must do our best to distinguish that which is time-bound from that which is timeless. Then, and only then, are we prepared for step three.

Step three: Homiletical Statement

How does it apply to me?

Only now are we ready to apply Scripture to the 21st century. Having performed the first two steps, we now have all that is needed to contextualize the principles to our own situation. Having worked the passage down to its basic principles, we must reengage these principles, properly applying our own culture and context.

For example, continuing with the head covering illustration, we must take the basic timeless principle and apply it to ourselves. In this case, here in 21st-century Norman, OK, head coverings or hats have no relevance to a woman's modesty. Sexually promiscuous dress today involves different things like the length of skirts and the height of tops. The principle of modesty still applies, just in other ways.

Again, this only applies to the ideas that have made it through all three steps of our process intact. Historical details, incidentals, and descriptive material will never have this type of immediate and practical application. Like with so much of Scripture, the primary application will be to believe it. I believe that God delivered the Israelites from bondage. It is a historical event that expresses God's faithfulness to his promises. Broadly speaking, I can use this as an illustration of God's faithfulness to his promises. But there is no reason for me to extract a timeless principle and say that God will deliver all people from all their pain in this life, and then apply it to my immediate situation saying God will deliver me from any difficulties I am going through. It is only the timeless principle that qualifies for timely application.

God has promised a lot of things. God has not promised a lot of things. So many times I want to read into Scripture promises he never actually made. I remember my mother did this before my sister Angie died. She read one of the Psalms about God's deliverance, and directly applied it to Angie's depression and her physical deliverance. It destroyed her when Angie died. She thought God had failed her.

It is so important for us to follow this process properly and faithfully. If we consistently interpret Scripture properly, we will be less prone to discouragement, disillusionment, and distancing ourselves from God. The Bible is so rich and full of application and information, but is not a magic book or a wax nose. It means what it means. Proper biblical interpretation, following the steps outlined above, will serve us well.

Suggested Reading for How to Study the Bible:

Living By the Book by William Hendricks (beginner)

How to Read the Bible for All its Word by Gordon Fee (intermediate)

The Hermeneutical Spiral by Grant Osborn

Notes:

APPENDIX B

ARGUMENTS FOR THE EXISTENCE OF GOD IN A NUTSHELL

1. Cosmological Argument: Also called the argument from universal causation or the argument from contingency, the cosmological argument is probably the most well-known and well-loved among theistic apologists. The basic argument is that all effects have an efficient cause. The universe, and all that is in it, due to its contingent (dependent) nature, is an effect. Therefore, the universe has a cause... but that cause cannot be an effect, or one would have to explain its cause. Therefore, there must be an ultimate cause, an unmoved mover, an uncaused cause that began the process. This cause must transcend time and space in order to transcend the law of cause and effect. This transcendent entity must be personal in order to willfully cause the effect. This ultimate cause is God.

2. Teleological Argument: (Gr. *telos*, "end" or "purpose") This is also known as the argument from design. This argument moves from complexity to a necessary explanatory cause for such complexity. The universe has definite design, order, and arrangement, which cannot be sufficiently explained outside a theistic worldview. From

APPENDIX B: ARGUMENTS FOR THE EXISTENCE OF GOD

the complexities of the human eye to the order and arrangement of the cosmology, the voice of God is heard. Therefore, God's existence is the best explanation for such design. God is the undesigned designer.

3. Moral Argument: This argument argues from the reality of moral laws to the existence of a necessary moral law giver. The idea here is that if there are moral laws (murder is wrong, selfishness is wrong, self-sacrifice is noble, torturing innocent babies for fun is evil), then there must be a transcendent explanation and justification for such laws. Otherwise, they are merely conventions that are not morally binding on anyone. Since there are moral laws, then there must be a moral law giver who transcends space and time. This moral law giver is God.

4. sensus divinitatus ("sense of the divine"): While this argument goes by many names, the *sensus divinitatus* argues for the existence of God from the innate sense of the divine that exists within humans. This sense of the divine, it can be argued, is the "God-shaped void" within all of us. This explains why people, societies, and cultures of all time have, by nature, sensed a need to worship something greater than themselves.

5. The Argument from Aesthetic Experience: This is the argument from universal beauty and pleasure. Beauty and pleasure are universally recognized as such. Even subjective variations in one's definition of what is beautiful are not distinct enough to relativize this principle. From the beauty of the sunset over the Rockies to the pleasure of eating certain foods, there is a common aesthetic experience that transcends the individual. This transcendence must have a ultimate source. This ultimate source is God.

6. Argument from the Existence of Arguments: The idea here is that there is no such thing as an argument without order and rationality. In the absence of God, all that exists is chaos. Chaos does not give birth to order. Arguments assume order. Order assumes purpose and design, which in turn require a transcendent being for their genesis. To even argue against the existence of God assumes his existence and is therefore self-referentially absurd. Therefore, there is no such thing as an "argument" against Transcendence (God).

7. Argument from the Existence of Free-will Arguments: If there is no God, then all we have is a meaningless series of cause and effect stretching back into eternity. This series of causes and effects is necessary and determined, being the result of the previous cause and effect. As a billiard ball is hit by another and has no self-motivated movements of its own, so all of human existence operates under the same conditions. All things are determined, not self-motivated, including beliefs. Therefore, if someone does not believe in God, it is not the result of self-motivated free-will beliefs, but because of a determined and fatalistic series of causes and effects stretching back into eternity. To argue against the existence of God would not be the result of looking at the evidence and making a more reasoned decision to not believe in God, but because that is what people were fatalistically determined to do. Therefore, all arguments are absurd and unjustified without God.

8. Argument from the Existence of Evil: Like the moral argument, this argument assumes the existence of a universal characteristic that is meaningless without God. Some argue that the existence of evil disproves God (or at least a good God), but to argue such is formally absurd since one would have to have an ultimate and transcendent standard of good in order to define evil. If evil exists, goodness exists. If both exist, there must be a transcendent norm from which they get their meaning. Since evil does exist, God exists.

9. Argument from Miracles: There are events in human history which cannot be explained outside of the existence of God. Many people have their subjective stories that bend them in the direction of theism, but there are also historical events, such as the resurrection of Christ and predictive prophecy, which cannot be explained without an acknowledgment of God. In short, from the Christian's standpoint, if Christ rose from the grave, then God exists. There is no alternative reasonable explanation that accounts for such an event outside a belief in God. History convincingly demonstrates that Christ did rise from the grave. Therefore, God exists.

APPENDIX B: ARGUMENTS FOR THE EXISTENCE OF GOD

10. Pascal's Wager: Popularized by French philosopher Blaise Pascal, Pascal's Wager argues that belief in God is the most rational choice due to the consequences of being wrong. If one were to believe in God and be wrong, there are no consequences. However, if one were to deny God and be wrong, the consequences are eternally tragic. Therefore, the most rational choice, considering the absence of *absolute* certainty, is not agnosticism or atheism (which one could *definitely* not be certain about), but a belief in God.

Suggested Reading for the Existence of God:

Evidence for God: 50 Arguments for Faith from the Bible, History, Philosophy, and Science by Mike Licona (editor)

Reasonable Faith by William Lane Craig

I Don't Have Enough Faith to be an Atheist by Norman Geisler and Frank Turek.

APPENDIX C

ARGUMENTS FOR THE RESURRECTION OF CHRIST IN A NUTSHELL

Just as we test the historicity of any event, not through emotional conviction, but with historical evidence, I would like to devote some time to laying out a brief historical case for the resurrection of Christ, the central tenet of the Christian faith. If Christ rose from the grave, it is all true and we just have to work out the details. If Christ did not rise from the grave, Christians are only to be pitied (1 Cor. 15:13-19).

Here is what we need.

Internal Evidence: Evidence coming from within the primary witness documents.

In this case, the primary witness documents are the twenty-seven works that make up what Christianity has traditionally called the New Testament. These works stand or fall individually from an historical standpoint. Therefore, they provide twenty-seven sources of documentation, not one.

APPENDIX C: ARGUMENTS FOR THE RESURRECTION

External Evidence: Collaborative evidence from outside the primary witness documents.

Some may include the non-Gospel works of the New Testament in this category. However, since most of these works were written by eyewitnesses of the events in question, it is correct to keep them primary.

Internal Evidence

- Honesty
- Irrelevant Details
- Harmony
- Public Extraordinary Claims
- Lack of Motivation for Fabrication

Honesty

A hallmark of embellishments and fabrications is that they display everyone in a positive light, only bringing to light their successes and triumphs. True history, on the other hand, will contain accounts that might cause some embarrassment.

The *entire* Bible records both the successes and failures of its heroes. I have always been impressed by this. It never paints the glorious picture you would expect from legendary material, but shows them in all their worst moments. The Israelites whined, David murdered, Peter denied, the apostles abandoned Christ in fear, Moses became angry, Jacob deceived, Noah got drunk, Adam and Eve disobeyed, Paul persecuted, Solomon worshiped idols, Abraham was a bigamist, Lot committed incest, John the Baptist doubted, Abraham doubted, Sarah doubted, Nicodemus doubted, Thomas doubted, Jonah ran, Samson self-served, and John, at the *very* end of the story, when he should have had it *all* figured out, worshiped an angel (Rev 22:8). I love it!

And these are the men and women who *wrote* the Bible!

In addition, the most faithful suffer the most (Joseph, Job, and Lazarus), while the wicked prosper (the rich man). In the case of the Gospels, the disciples who wrote them abandoned Christ and did not believe His resurrection when told of it. Even after the resurrection, they still presented themselves as completely ignorant of God's plan (Acts 1:6-7). Women were the first witnesses to the resurrection, which has an element of self-incrimination since a woman's testimony was not worth much in the first century. If someone were making this up, why include such an incriminating detail? (I am glad they did – what an Easter message this is for us today!)

(The primary departure from this, although in the OT, is in 1 and 2 Chronicles, which do hide some of King David's failures. Even then, the accounts are not promising for Israel as a whole).

One last thing I think belongs in this category: None of the Gospel writers gave their names. In other words, the reason we believe Matthew, Mark, Luke, and John (two disciples and two colleagues of the disciples) wrote the Gospels is due to early tradition. Even John simply refers to himself as "the one whom Jesus loved." Initial reaction is one of skepticism (even though the traditions are very early). Why didn't they include their names? However, from another historical perspective, this is a significant mark of genuineness. The M.O. of the day was to write pseudepigrapha. Pseudepigrapha are writings that seek to gain credibility by falsely attributing their work to another of more prominent stature. It would be like me writing a book, but saying it was by Chuck Swindoll in order to sell more copies. Pseudepigrapha normally came hundreds of years after the death of the supposed author. However, since the Gospel writers did not include their names, it demonstrates that they were not following this model of fabrication. This actually adds another mark of historical credibility. Why would they leave their names out if what they wrote was fabricated? If these works were not really by them, they would have no hope of acceptance.

Irrelevant Details

The Gospel writers (especially John) include many elements to their stories that are really irrelevant to the big picture. Normally, when someone is making up a story, they include only the details that contribute to the fabrication. Irrelevant details are a mark of genuineness in all situations.

Notice this small segment of the Gospel of John 20:1-8 (adapted from Gregory Boyd, *Letters to a Skeptic*):

"Early on the first day of the week (when? does it matter?), while it was still dark (who cares?), Mary Magdalene (an incriminating detail) went to the tomb and saw that the stone had been removed from the entrance. So she came running to Simon Peter and the other disciple, the one who Jesus loved (John's modest way of referring to himself – another mark of genuineness) and said, "They have taken the Lord out of the tomb and we don't know where they have taken him!" (note her self-incriminating lack of faith here). So Peter and the other disciple started for the tomb. They were running, but the other disciple outran Peter and reached the tomb first (who cares who won the race? a completely irrelevant detail). He bent over (irrelevant, but the tomb entrance was low – a detail which is historically accurate of wealthy people's tombs at the time – the kind we know Jesus was buried in) and looked in at the strips of linen lying there but did not go in (why not? irrelevant detail). Then Simon Peter, who was behind him, arrived and went into the tomb (Peter's boldness stands out in all the Gospel accounts). He saw the strips of linen lying there, as well as the burial cloth that had been around Jesus' head (irrelevant and unexpected detail – what was Jesus wearing?). The cloth was folded up by itself, separate from the linen (somewhat irrelevant and unusual. Jesus folded one part of his wrapping before he left!). Finally the other disciple, who reached the tomb first, also went inside (who cares about what exact order they went in?)

The best example I can think of is the polar bear. What? Okay, only those of you who watched the television series *Lost* will get this. In the first season, there was a polar bear in the show. We all wondered why it was there on the island. How did it get there? What was the meaning of the polar bear? How was it going to fit into the big picture? These are all legitimate questions that many of us sat on the edge of our seats for five seasons waiting to get the answers to. However, the polar bear (along with so many other incidentals) was never explained. There was a great outcry because there were so many questions left unanswered. So many irrelevant details remained irrelevant. The reason why the outcry was legitimate was because in fictional (or fabricated) stories, details are *never* irrelevant. They are written into the script and have a purpose that supports the whole of the fictional story. However, if the show *Lost* were not fictional but historical, the irrelevant details would be expected. True history does not have to work itself out into a paradigm of the story arch. The presence of irrelevant details, while not conclusive, does speak to the historicity of the story.

Harmony

The four Gospel writers claim to have witnessed the resurrected Christ. The same is the case for most of the other writers of the NT. The four Gospel writers all write of the same event from differing perspectives. Although they differ in details, they are completely harmonious regarding the main details surrounding the resurrection, and all claim it was an historical event.

Many people are disturbed by the seeming disharmony among the Gospels, since the Gospel writers do not include all the same details. However, this is actually a mark of historicity, since if they all said exactly the same thing, it would be a sign that they had collaborated prior to writing their accounts. However, the Gospels contain just enough disharmony to give them a mark of genuine historicity.

Public Extraordinary Claims

The Bible records that the resurrection of Christ happened and gives the time, place, people involved, and the names of many witnesses. In other

APPENDIX C: ARGUMENTS FOR THE RESURRECTION

words, the extraordinary events did not occur in secret, as would be the case if the story were fabricated. Look to all the ancient myths and you will see how obscure the mythology has to be in order to claim historicity. Why? Because if you give too many details of times, people, and places, the myths can be easily disproven. If the resurrection was a fabrication, the author would have said only one person knew about it. He should have said it happened in a cave or a place no one has ever heard of. There are numerous religions started by those types of stories.

This graphic caused quite a stir when I originally published it:

How Christianity Started

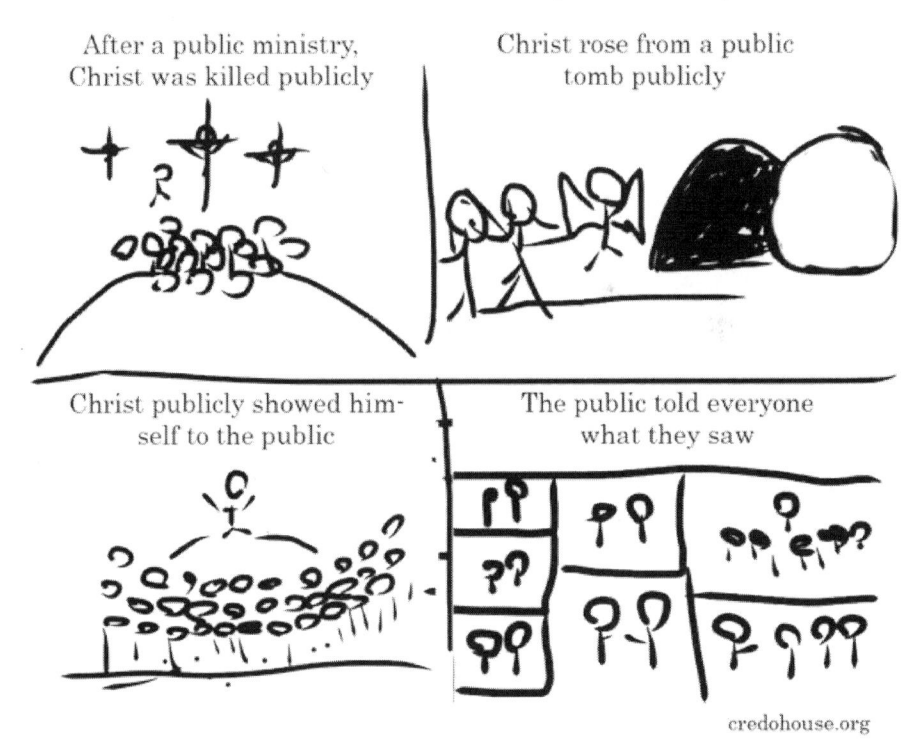

After a public ministry, Christ was killed publicly

Christ rose from a public tomb publicly

Christ publicly showed himself to the public

The public told everyone what they saw

credohouse.org

How Other Religions Started

Private dream about God

OR

Private angelic encounter about God

OR

Private idea about God

One person told everyone what he saw

As Paul says to King Agrippa, "For the king knows about these matters [concerning the resurrection of Christ], and I speak to him also with confidence, since I am persuaded that none of these things escape his notice; for this has not been done in a corner." (Act 26:26)

Lack of Motive for Fabrication

There is no *reasonable* explanation as to why the Apostles (or anyone for that matter) would have made up such a story. They had no popularity, power, or riches to gain from it if it was a lie. They were constantly persecuted because of their confession, and most met terrible ends, sealing their testimony in blood.

Beyond this, it was culturally unacceptable at *all* levels to have a crucified

APPENDIX C: ARGUMENTS FOR THE RESURRECTION

and resurrected Messiah. The Jews certainly were not expecting their Messiah to be crucified. The Greek world would have nothing but disdain for the idea of a bodily resurrection since, from their perspective, the material body was something from which we desire to escape. Therefore, for this story to arise at *this time in history* would have been about the most counterproductive story anyone could have made up!

It could not have been an illusion, for illusions do not happen en masse, over time. It could not have been a case of mistaken identity (i.e., they merely thought they saw Christ), since it is impossible to explain how so many witnesses could be mistaken about seeing someone dead and buried, and then seeing the same person alive three days later. It could not be that Christ did not really die, since the Romans were expert executioners, and many people helped wrap Christ in his burial cloths, as was their custom. It is very unlikely that it was made up, since all the objectors (and there were plenty of them!) had to do was produce a body.

External Evidence

While internal evidence looks to the evidence coming from inside the primary witness documents, external evidence seeks to find collaborative evidence coming from *outside* the primary witness documents.

For the resurrection of Christ, I submit this line of external evidence:

- Preservation of the Documents

- Archeology

- Extra-biblical Attestation

- Survival in a Hostile Environment

Preservation of the Documents

This has to do with the manuscript evidence of the New Testament, the primary source documents concerning the resurrection. While we don't have any of the originals in our possession (nor should we expect to), the manuscript evidence for the New Testament is very strong. According to renowned textual scholar Daniel Wallace, "We have an embarrassment of riches." Not only do we have hundreds of manuscripts that date before the fifth century (some from as far back as the second and third), we also have many quotations from the early church fathers that alone could be used to reconstruct most of the New Testament. All of this tells us that the accounts we read are essentially the same as the accounts that were originally given. While there are some differences among the manuscripts, even Bart Ehrman, former Fundamentalist, textual scholar, and critic of Christianity, says that no major doctrine is affected by the differences, and that most are very insignificant.

In addition, and very significantly, the manuscript evidence tells us that the Gospel accounts of the resurrection were all written within a generation of the events they record, giving evidence for their claims to be eyewitness testimony. There was not enough time for legendary material to arise.

Archaeology

The witness of archaeology has continually confirmed the scriptural data. When there has been doubt in the past about the Gospel accounts (e.g., date of the Gospel of John, etc.), later archaeological and historical finds seem to always confirm the historical accuracy of Scripture.

Jewish archaeologist Nelson Glueck says about the Bible, "It may be stated categorically that no archaeological discovery has ever controverted a biblical reference. Scores of archaeological findings have been made which confirm in clear outline or in exact detail historical statements in the Bible. And, by the same token, proper evaluation of biblical descriptions has often led to amazing discoveries." (Nelson Glueck *Rivers in the Desert; History of*

Negev [Philadelphia: Jewish Publications Society of America, 1969], 31).

Sir William Ramsay is regarded as one of the greatest archaeologists ever to have lived. As an atheist, he set out to disprove the historical accuracy of the Scriptures. However, after researching the writings of Luke (the books of Luke and Acts), he changed his mind. He became a firm defender of Christianity and the historical accuracy of the Gospel accounts. About Luke he wrote, "Luke is a historian of the first rank; not merely are his statements of fact trustworthy…this author should be placed along with the very greatest historians."

As well, it cannot be overlooked that Christ's remains were never found. This is an issue of archaeology. Combined with the understanding that Christianity arose very early under the claim of Christ's resurrection, and that there were many detractors, the archaeological evidence of the empty tomb is important. Those who denied the resurrection in the first century could not produce a body (much less can those who deny it today). This is a necessary precondition to collaborate the evidence of such a belief.

Extra-Biblical Attestation

Over 39 extra-biblical sources attest to more than 100 facts regarding the life and teachings of Jesus. Besides all of the early Apostolic Fathers (whose witness cannot be dismissed simply because they believed that Christ was the Messiah), we have Jewish and Roman historians.

There are numerous first- and second-century extra-biblical writers who testify to the fact that Christians believed Christ did extraordinary things, died on a cross, and rose from the grave: Josephus, Clement, Papias, Didache, Barnabas, Justin Martyr, Ignatius, Irenaeus, Hermas, Tatian, Theophilus, Athenagoras, Clement of Alexandria.

In reality, though, "extra-biblical attestation" is not really the best term for this line of evidence. Really, it should be "collaborative attestation" since we are not looking for attestation that is outside the Bible or even the New

Testament, but for collaborative evidence outside the document that is under historical investigation. *Therefore, the New Testament itself provides more than enough collaborative support for the events of the resurrection, since each of the twenty-seven documents must be seen as pieces of individual evidence that stand on their own.* As I said at the beginning, there is no reason to put them together in a single corpus called "the New Testament" and say that the corpus must find its own collaborative support. Mark supports Luke. John supports Matthew. Paul supports Acts. The point is that every New Testament book individually provides very strong collaborative evidence for the historicity of the resurrection.

As a side note, I am amused by those who demand that Christians produce "secular" support for the resurrection (defining "secular" as "from those who are not believers"). It is as if those who did believe in the resurrection should get less credit than those who did not believe in it. It would be like saying that in order for me to believe in the assassination of John F. Kennedy, I have to have evidence from those who do not believe that he was assassinated, and that those who do not believe it are more credible than those who do. However, as in the case of the resurrection, if it truly happened, then we would expect the closest people to the evidence to believe it rather than not believe it. Therefore, to deem "secular" or "skeptical" support as necessary and more trustworthy evidence is a bias that is too bent to come to objective conclusions.

Survival in a Hostile Environment

The very fact that Christianity survived, even with such public and extraordinary truth claims, is offered as a line of external evidence. That Christianity had its hostile objectors is supported by all the evidence, internal and external. The objectors to Christianity had every opportunity to expose the fabrication of the resurrection if it were truly a fabrication. The fact that those who were hostile to Christianity did not put forth a substantial or unified case against it adds to its historicity.

According to Gregory Boyd, "Christianity was born in a very hostile environment. There were contemporaries who would have refuted the Gospel portrait of Jesus – if they could have. The leaders of Judaism in the first century saw Christianity as a pernicious cult and would have loved to see it stamped out. And this would have been easy to do – if the 'cult' had been based on fabrications. Why, just bringing forth the body of the slain Jesus would have been sufficient to extinguish Christianity once and for all. In spite of this, however, Christianity exploded. . . . Even those who remained opposed to Christianity did not deny that Jesus did miracles, and did not deny that His tomb was empty." (Gregory Boyd, *Letters from a Skeptic* [Colorado Springs, CO: Cook Communication Ministries, 2003], 85-86).

Considering the internal and external arguments for the resurrection of Christ, I don't ask anyone to look to just one of these lines of evidence alone, but to consider the cumulative case. It is very strong. If the resurrection indeed occurred, it would be hard to expect more evidence. In fact, what we would expect is *exactly* what we have.

Of course, alternatives to each one of these could be (and have been) offered. Alternatives to many other well-established historical events have been offered, including the Holocaust, the landing on the moon, and the death of Elvis. However, in most cases, the alternatives go against the obvious. In the end, all other alternatives for the resurrection, while possible, are completely improbable and require a greater leap of faith than does just believing Christ rose from the grave. The simplest explanation is always the best. The simplest explanation to the data here is that Christ *did* rise from the grave. Those who deny the resurrection do so not on the basis of the evidence, but because they have other presuppositions which don't allow them to believe. The historical evidence is simply too strong.

I believe any objective historian can look to the evidence for the resurrection of Christ and conclude that he is indeed risen.

Suggested Reading for the Resurrection of Christ:

Who Moved the Stone by Frank Morison

The Case for the Resurrection of Jesus by Gary Habermas and Mike Licona

The Case for Easter by Lee Strobel

Faith

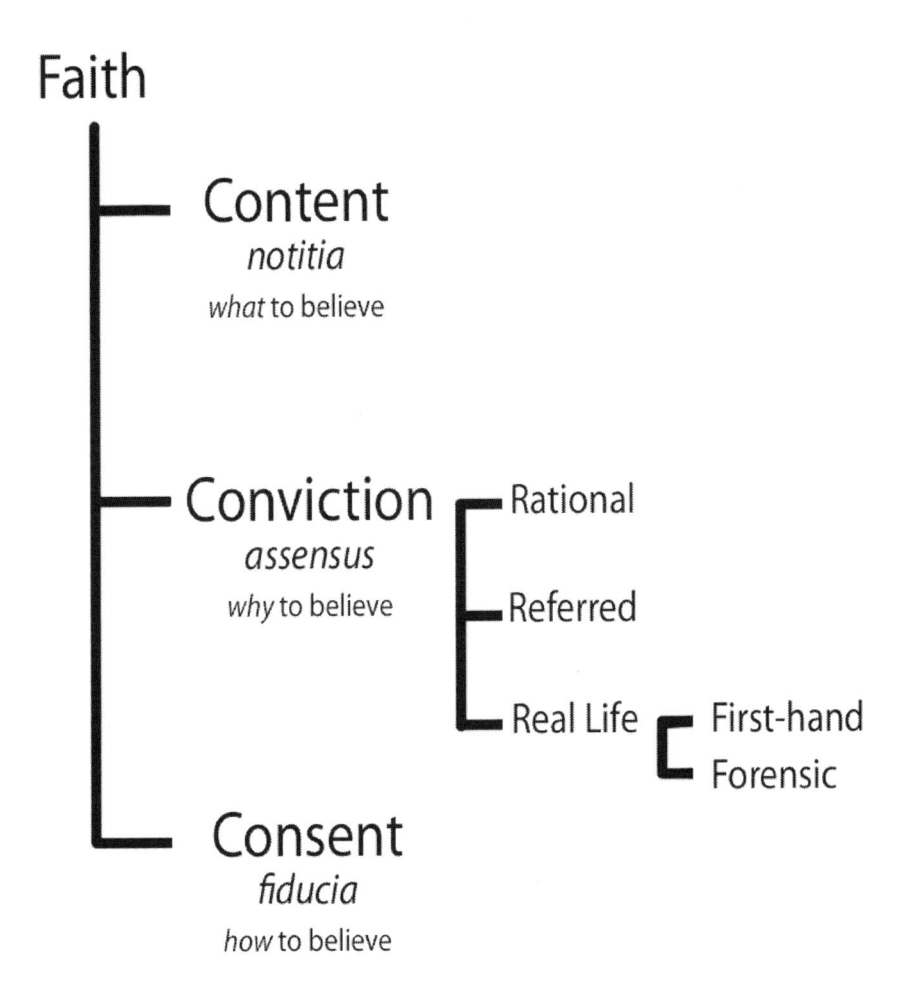

- ## Content
  notitia
  what to believe

- ## Conviction
  assensus
  why to believe
  - Rational
  - Referred
  - Real Life
    - First-hand
    - Forensic

- ## Consent
  fiducia
  how to believe

Made in the USA
San Bernardino, CA
09 February 2014